Bill Mitchell's Yorkshire

COMPILED BY DAVID MITCHELL

Dalesman

First published in 2016 by Dalesman, an imprint of Country Publications Ltd
The Water Mill, Broughton Hall, Skipton, North Yorkshire BD23 3AG
www.dalesman.co.uk

Text © WR Mitchell 2016
Additional material © David Mitchell 2016
Pictures © WR Mitchell and other copyright holders 2016

ISBN 978-1-85568-354-9

Typeset in Goudy Old Style.

Printed in China by 1010 Printing International Ltd.

Contents

FOREWORD..5

INTRODUCTION...8

FAMILY AND ROOTS
Life in't back street: Skipton in the austere 1930s.......................................12
A Yorkshire courtship..14
From the Yorkshire Dales to Salt Lake City...16
Looking for Grandad..18

HERALDING A CAREER FOR THE DALESMAN
Ink on my fingers..19
A Dales editor...22
Tales of a dryland sailor..24
Homely beginnings with the great Scotts..26

PEOPLE BEFORE THINGS
Old Mick the bull walloper..29
Annie Mason...32
Dalesfolk I remember: Bill Alderson..34
Dalesfolk I remember: Kit Calvert..36
Hannah's Christmas...41
Life and times of Tot Lord..43
Tot Tommy..45
Tommy Moore: the complete dalesman..46
Sally's parrot...48

FAR FROM THE MADDING CROWD
Sad day as bus company completes its final journey.....................................49
A postman's life...52
A taste of some old-fashioned medicine...55
A Dales tailor..56
Broadcasting in the Broad Acres..58
Tales about babyhood..60

TRADITIONS
Showtime at Muker..61
Dancing in the Dales...64
Last of the 'terrible' knitters..66
Dales tales of a Christmas past..68
First footing at White Scar...71
Lecturer's magic lantern effect that brought nature to life............................72

YORKSHIRE'S SCENIC VARIETY
White walls of Yorkshire..73
Nineteen forty-seven...77

Tour brings thoughts of the past...79
Shuttle service to the underworld..81
Drystone walls add to Dales landscape...83
A corner of Yorkshire: Goathland...86
Ilkley Moor Baht 'at...87
A corner of Yorkshire: Janet's Foss...89

HISTORY
Looking for Lady Anne..90
The Romantics and the Dales...94

ARTS
JB in the Dales...95
Great-great Grandad knew the Brontës..97
Young Mr Herriot..99
Christopher Timothy on location..103
Cutcliffe Hyne: a huge man, mentally and physically........................105
Chapters in a Dales life...107
Elgar's friendship with a Yorkshire doctor..111
The clouds are mucky: Ashley Jackson..112
Fred Lawson..116
Thelma Barlow..117

WILDLIFE/NATURE
Richard Kearton...118
Legacy of Yorkshire's natural history boys...120
Evenings with barn owls...123
The farming family who built up a stock of deer.................................125
Gardening's own rock legend...127

THERE'S METHODISM IN MY MADNESS
Pulpit tales of the Yorkshire Dales...129
Old-style Methodism...130
Mr Parker's favourite hymn...132

SUFFERING FROM SETTLE-CARLITIS
The railway in the clouds..134
The runaway..135
A quest for the shanties...138
When the Scots Express left the rails..143
Dalesfolk I remember: Harry Secombe..144

CLIMB EVERY MOUNTAIN...
Coast to Coast...146
Cleveland Way..149

My Yorkshire... WR MITCHELL...155

ACKNOWLEDGEMENTS...157

PAGE REFERENCES...157

Foreword by Bill Mitchell

Forty-five years ago, I sauntered into the Royal Oak Hotel at Settle, intent on interviewing Owd Mick, one of the last of the Dales drovers – a man known locally as a 'bull walloper'. It was to be my first article on joining Harry Scott at *The Dalesman*. Mick's main claim to fame was his reputed ability to drink twelve pints of ale to twelve strokes of the clock. An old injury to his throat meant that he no longer

Bill at a book-signing event

had to waste valuable drinking time in gulping. I don't think that anyone saw him live up to his reputation but he was kept well supplied with ale by curious visitors. I subsidised Mick to the extent of five pints. Since that article was published, Mick has 'gone to his rest' (buried in the part of Giggleswick churchyard 'where there's a tree and I can hear the birds sing.') and I have contributed to *The Dalesman* over a million words about Yorkshire and its people.

This county is vast and varied. At its heart is York Minster, built of Tadcaster limestone, complementing the chalk of the Wolds – a crescent of chalk extending from south of the Humber to a dramatic termination in the white cliffs of Bempton and Flamborough. Further north, the sea cliffs are grand but darker in hue, the north-east hinterland being dominated by the North York Moors – a hundred thousand acres of heather and bogland, grooved by small valleys which the Norsefolk called dales. Westwards are the Pennines, Defoe's 'wall of brass'.

Yorkshire folk are as varied as the terrain. They are bound to each other by county pride. Yorkshire fishermen sail the short, sharp sea off the north-east coast in cobles, which at other times lie on an open beach. The coble has been described as 'boat and harbour in one'. Yorkshire miners inhabit pit villages, some of which are ringed by cornfields. Yorkshire milltowners inhabit stone forests and the cricketers in white flannels stand out against the dark shades of old factories. The Dales farmer, with crook in hand and dog at foot, bestrides a broad Pennine fellside while attending to his sheep.

Yorkshire's beauty is more than skin deep, as the explorers of caves and potholes in the north-west will testify. The main chamber of Gaping Gill has a scale to rival York Minster. Motoring from my home at Giggleswick to the cliffs overlooking the North Sea – and travelling against the grain of the landscape – I have marvelled at the contrasting scenes. There has been the thrill of personal discovery – the remains of old abbeys and the half-forgotten villages tucked away in folds between the hills. I recall with special pleasure my encounters with Yorkshire folk who are so varied in their speech, manners and occupations and yet are united by a love for their native county.

There's none better.

Bill Mitchell

Introduction by David Mitchell

I often thought that Dad and I would make a formidable quiz team: I could provide the sporting knowledge and he could do the rest. Despite leaving school early, he had a thirst for knowledge in his young days and made himself an authority on many subjects by observing, listening and enquiring. His range of expertise was remarkable, a veritable A to Z. This celebratory book focuses on

Bill and wife Freda with their children, Janet and David

his Yorkshire-related output across a distinguished career. A number of pieces are being published for the first time.

Dad's thundering typewriter was an abiding image from my childhood. Close up the vibrations could be felt as he pounded through yet another book or article. His office was based in the attic of 4 High Hill Grove, 'down t'snicket by t' post office', in Settle. The room was also my bedroom! Above the desk, the ceiling was 'decorated' by a yellow ring created over the years by his addiction to nicotine. Dad was never far from a cigarette.

I often thumbed through the books that lined his study walls and was sufficiently inspired to consider a career in journalism. However, my ideal job was far removed from anything Dad would have felt comfortable with. Working as a sports writer for the *Daily Telegraph* would have been intolerable for a man who found it difficult to match my love for everything connected with a ball. Dad had reported on local football for the *Craven Herald* when footballs weighed a ton and shorts and socks met somewhere round the knee, but admitted to me many times that he waited for something exciting to happen before nudging his next-door spectator to find out what.

We shared few sporting moments but, to be fair, he did make regular trips to Burnley's Turf Moor to satisfy my childhood enthusiasm for the Claret and Blues. His favourite time in the game, apart from the final whistle, was when the afternoon drew on and the lights of Burnley started to twinkle all around.

He also provided bowling for my constant batting practice in the back yard at High Hill Grove. He was left-arm medium-pace with a style which could best be described as busy. A box of matches rattled regularly in his pocket as he ran up. He bowled in short spells as I recall and I relied on my mother, who was no mean player in her time (appearing for Johnson and Johnson at Gargrave), to put the hours in. After all, she had more time to devote to preparing her son as the next Geoffrey Boycott. Dad was always busy.

The only sport which absorbed his attention, bizarrely, was wrestling on ITV at five to four every Saturday afternoon. In those days there were proper sports programmes on Saturdays. He would watch avidly as Mick McManus, Billy Two Rivers and others would wrestle each other to submission in front of live audiences around the country. I waited patiently to turn over as soon as possible to watch the teleprinter bring in the football results on Grandstand with David Coleman.

During my last year at school Dad and I talked about journalism as a career. He suggested that I tried to get a place on a local paper, preferably the *Craven Herald* in Skipton. I also needed to enrol at college. So it was, in January 1973, that he cleared snow from around the car before taking me to Preston for an interview at Harris College. It was a tortuous journey, as I recall. Not only did we get there safely but I was offered a place. All was looking good until I had a change of heart a couple of months later, deciding that it was an unpredictable choice of career and opted to become a teacher. This was a wholly more reliable job, or so I thought.

I retired in 2009 after three headships and two redundancies. At fifty-five, I had plenty of time to achieve long-cherished ambitions and writing was at the top of the list. As I set out to write my own books, Dad was always there with sound advice. The importance of an eye-catching title, for instance. One that particularly sticks was his insistence that the opening line had impact. It must draw the reader in straight away.

Alongside this new pursuit,

Bill and Freda

I also carried out voluntary press work at Fleetwood Town Football Club. This covered a range of journalistic assignments so, ironically, the profession that I had tossed aside all those years ago was now providing satisfaction in retirement. Each article that I sent to Dad was dutifully pasted into his scrapbook diaries. All sixty-three volumes have now found their way to my house.

Dad kept a close interest in all that I did and was particularly fascinated by modern methods used to produce my books. He was familiar with a computer, and the cut-and-paste facility was a great improvement on the laborious typewriter where there was less room for error. However, he found it difficult to understand how complete manuscripts could be sent by telephone or kept on a memory stick the length of his finger. He marvelled at the use of social media to publicise books.

In the last period of his life he was to see such up-to-date methods applied to his own books. He wrote a series which, although short in length, was each very personal in its own way. The books were intended for family and friends and helped to fill a large gap in his life following the death of Freda in 2007. Life with Freda was recalled in *A Yorkshire Courtship*. *Life In't Back Street* showed the clarity of his long-term memory as he went back to the 1930s, growing up in Skipton. *Pulpit Tales* featured stories from his time as a Methodist preacher. *From the Yorkshire Dales to Salt Lake City* told a fascinating story of how some of Mum's ancestors travelled from a farming life in the Dales to the middle of America in the 1800s.

Dad, though well into his eighties, was still able to be energised by a subject and to construct a manuscript in a remarkably short time. He was also still remarkably adept at proofreading. I was able to facilitate the production and marketing through 'modern methods', even setting up his own Twitter account.

In his diaries, Dad recalls the arrival of *A Yorkshire Courtship*, in July 2011:

'The support being given by David and Janet in preparing for publication my record of courtship years with Freda is much appreciated. I've been publishing all my working life but remain impressed by the way the copy and pictures for *A Yorkshire Courtship* are being transformed into stylish book form using ultra-modern methods.'

I hope that you enjoy reading this selection of evocative pieces from a distinguished career.

David Mitchell

Family and Roots

Life in't back street: Skipton in the austere 1930s

I was born in Skipton in 1928 and grew up during the lean years of the 1930s. Apart from Sundays or holidays the town lay in a grey murk of smoke from half a dozen mills. Now and again, with a change of wind, the air would clear. When a fickle wind changed direction again the street might be blotted out by noxious-smelling smoke. Local folk talked splutteringly in a visibility reduced to a few yards. T' back street vanished from view every wash day when lengths of cord were stretched from one side to the other. Newly washed sheets and clothes were draped from them using wooden pegs and props. T'newspaper lad, arriving at the head of the street on washday, had a heavy shop-bike. On one day, he lost control. The bike ran through three lines of washing before coming to a halt lodged against a wall.

The Saturday afternoon activity of our local gang depended on the matinee we had seen at the local cinema. Cowboys and Indians were favourites. The Indian bows and arrows were made from redundant canes slyly taken from local allotments. If the film was about the Foreign Legion, the front wall of a garden became a desert fort. Capstones might come loose during an attack by Arabs. The garden owner was not amused. On one occasion when playing an army game I got one of Mum's baking tins stuck on my head when it was doubling as a helmet. She tried without success to remove it and I was whisked up the road to the local hospital for professional help!

Bill as a boy

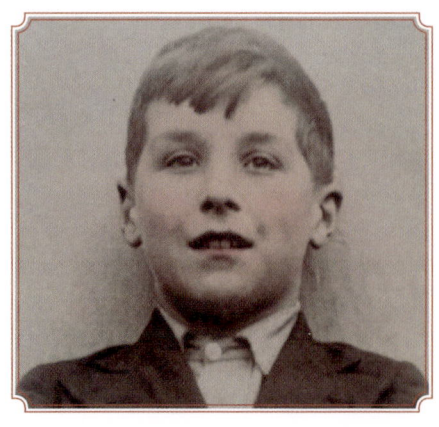

Above: A young Bill with his mother and sister
Below: The next generation – Bill with children
David and Janet at an awards cermony

A Yorkshire courtship

The story of a wonderful marriage became a firm favourite of Dad's. It was a loving tribute that touched many hearts. For many it brought back memories of their own marriages as they grew up through similar times.

My heartbeat quickened when I met Freda. Buses came prominently into our working lives. Freda used a green-sided 'Laycock's' bus for part of her journey to work from West Marton to Gargrave. My workaday bus, twixt Skipton and Clapham, was bright orange and bore the name 'Pennine'. Cupid set to work one murky November day. I had been working late and so, it turned out, had Freda.

When my bus reached Gargrave and Freda clambered aboard, there was only one spare seat – next to me. She occupied it. We smiled at each other. We exchanged pleasantries. In the ten minutes twixt Gargrave and Skipton I had a John Wesley experience, though in a different context. My heart was 'strangely warmed'. Freda might have recognised me from a recent dance, at which my companion had been a somewhat staid young woman who, I suspected, was more interested in dancing than in me.

Freda now wanted to know why I should be travelling on a late bus to Skipton. I told her I had completed some extra work at Clapham, home of *The Dalesman*. 'I'm fifty per cent of the editorial staff'. Why had I not seen her on the bus before? She had been working late and had to travel home by a devious route. I lightened the conversation with a question made famous in a series of radio programmes featuring Wilfred Pickles: 'Are you courting?' We both laughed. Silence except for the roar of the bus engine. 'Are you courting?' The question hung in the air for a while. Freda blushed a little – and shook her head. Neither was I. Her shopping trips from a farmhouse in West Marton to Skipton High Street were usually in the company of her mother. They shopped, then dined at the Castle Café which stood at the head of the High Street. I somewhat recklessly asked Freda, a new acquaintance, if one day I could take over her Mum's role and entertain her to tea at her favourite café. There was a slight colouring of her cheeks. She thought about my proposition as the bus journey drew to a halt. Before we parted, she for another bus, me to walk home, she nodded her head. We parted smiling.

Bill and Freda, the happy couple

From the Yorkshire Dales to Salt Lake City

Whereas Dad's family had, like countless others, moved from country to town in the Industrial Revolution, Mum's had developed as Yorkshire farmers. Matthew and Jane Bell were converted by Mormon missionaries from the New World, operating from a base in Preston, and embarked on a long and hazardous journey to the valley of the Great Salt Lake in Utah. It was January 1852.

Matthew and Jane, in an alien environment, stared with creaky necks at the ship's rigging which seemed to tickle the sky. The sea was far from calm. Within a day or so, most of the passengers were sea-sick. A child who died was buried at sea. A few prayers were uttered before the body of the luckless infant was laid to rest, wrapped in a sheet, with a weight to ensure it would not float. The body of the little fellow had been tipped from a wide board – and was gone.

Matthew and Jane spent some time on deck, enjoying the fresh air and listening to the slapping of water against the wooden hull of the boat. They then went below, occupying part of a bench that, with others, flanked a long table handy to their chosen bunks, each six feet in length, eighteen inches wide. Ten cubic feet was allocated for luggage, passengers having been advised to leave in the ship's hold anything that was not immediately necessary. There were sanitation problems. Disease was likely to spread. Some of the sailors were lustful. Life was generally tedious with the novelty, for Matthew and Jane, of being out of sight of land.

The ocean was in a kindly mood until there was a dramatic change in a ten-day period from 14th January. The ship was overtaken by a hurricane and with a large quantity of railroad iron on board, it rolled heavily. Passengers packed like sardines wailed and grunted. Huddled below deck with the wind howling through the rigging, Matthew and Jane had to tolerate conditions that were crowded and noisy. They had little more than biscuits and cold water. The ship stank, despite the regular cleaning of living quarters. A nervous Jane grasped Matthew's hand ever more tightly. Deaths were reported. In most people's minds was the risk of disease. Two children were born.

Another died. A couple were married and Jane discovered she was expecting a baby.

Spirits were revived, and cheers were heard, when the ship came within sight of a lighthouse at the mouth of the Mississippi. Cheers turned to moans when the vessel slurred to a halt on the mudbar of this mighty river. On 11th March, a tug was available to take the Mormon immigrants 120 miles up river to New Orleans. Glancing at the shore of the New World, Matthew dubbed it a 'curious sort of land'. His past life had been spent amid purple-headed hills dotted with sheep and multi-toned meadows mown by a scythe. The area he viewed from the river looked barren, incapable of sustaining cattle. Then, surprised, he located several healthy-looking herds grazing near the water's edge. More positive signs of civilization were houses, gardens and trees. The Yorkshire couple clung on to each other and spoke excitedly as the steamboat left a V-shaped pattern on the Mississippi. Matthew, born beside the infant River Wharfe, was impressed to learn that the course of the American river was well over three thousand miles.

RMS Europa, a transatlantic steamer pictured in the 1850s

Looking for Grandad

Grandad was a stocky man who, when wearing a waistcoat, would adorn it with watch, chain and medallion. This was a fad at the time. Grandad, as I remember him, was thin on top (as was Dad and also me!) and, unlike us, had a bushy moustache. He had an impediment in his speech, an initial letter S becoming T. He was married to Telina!

Everyone in the village of Bradley knew his place and when Grandad and Dad were sacked from the main mill they simply walked to Skipton for work. After working through the day at Skipton, Grandad attended evening meetings at the Weavers' Institute. He was a great Union man. During the General Strike in the 1920s when there was no transport he kept a preaching appointment at Grassington by walking there and back. He had blistered feet for his troubles while the soles of his worn-out shoes were flapping!

Grandad's only weakness was smoking a pipe. One weekend, when a visiting minister was given board and lodging, Grandad did not want to offend him by smoking. He paid a sly daytime visit to his bedroom, high above ground.

Opening the window, he lit up the pipe. Smoke was dispersed in the great outdoors. He glanced at the garden. The minister, standing near the toilet that was situated at the end of a garden path, was puffing away at a briar!

The last I saw of Grandad was as he lay in his coffin in the main bedroom. I recall a general greyness, grey face and grey moustache. He did not leave much, just a few books on a high shelf and some jottings. He was a keen writer who had many good tales about weavers and accounts of visits to Brontë land published in newspapers.

Lights Out

An old Dalesman lay ill in his remote cottage. He said to his wife, 'I think I'm dying. Just light me a candle for my last hours.'

'But do ye know t' price o' candles?' replied his wife.

Eventually she gave in. 'All reet, I'll light you a candle. But if you feel yourself going, blow it out.'

Heralding a Career for the Dalesman

Ink on my fingers

Dad's working life began at the Craven Herald *newspaper on Skipton High Street. It was to be a connection that lasted through his life, his last article being published on the day his death was announced.*

On a sunlit day in the mid-1940s I arrived at the offices of the *Craven Herald & Pioneer* in Skipton – the latest recruit to their reporting staff which was now boosted to three. John Mitchell, editor-manager, told me that I was lucky. The last cub reporter to be appointed paid for his training. Times had changed. I would receive a wage – 12s 6d a week.

Bill at his typewriter

MONTHLY   THE   SIXPENCE

DALESMAN

THE HEADLAND, SCARBOROUGH by Dan Binns

NUMBER FIVE   **VOLUME TWELVE**

AUGUST 1950

THE FESTIVAL OF BRITAIN - THE LUPIN MAN
STARTING A MOORLAND SMALLHOLDING
FAMILY LIFE OF THE CURLEW - YOUTH HOSTEL NEWS

Whirlwind in the Top Meadow - Heard in a Dales 'Bus

A Village in Malhamdale - Yorkshire Parish Councils

Dales Farmer's Diary - With the Young Farmers

A Beekeeper's Notebook - Readers' Club

The reporter's room on the top floor was as bare as a prison cell. A fireplace imparted heat and warmed the meat pies which, as youngest reporter, I collected at mid-morning from Mr Bean's shop in Middle Row. Everywhere were flakes of yellowing newsprint from bound copies of old newspapers used for reference.

At mid-morning we were joined by sub-editor Harry Scott, who, in 1939, brought out the first copy of *The Yorkshire Dalesman*. The war led to paper rationing and other controls. Harry must augment his income on the weekly newspaper. He had walked one and a half miles from Clapham village to the station, avoiding a drove of semi-wild horses that roamed Newby Moor, and at Skipton had another good walk to the office. As he entered, the door slammed behind him, having been fitted with a length of cord and a lead weight. His first words to me were 'Hail to thee, blithe spirit'. It marked him out as someone special.

On my first visit to Settle, by bus, I contacted our local correspondent, Hector Renshaw, who spent most of his day standing at the door of an outfitter's shop. We had news correspondents in every village. The Misses Seed of Dent neatly sewed together the pages of copy.

Our friend, Sam Stables, of Grassington, just scribbled a few words. He reported that 'an albino crow has been seen in Upper Wharfedale'. We spiked the sheet which meant it could not be used. Sam repeated the story

Bill's press card

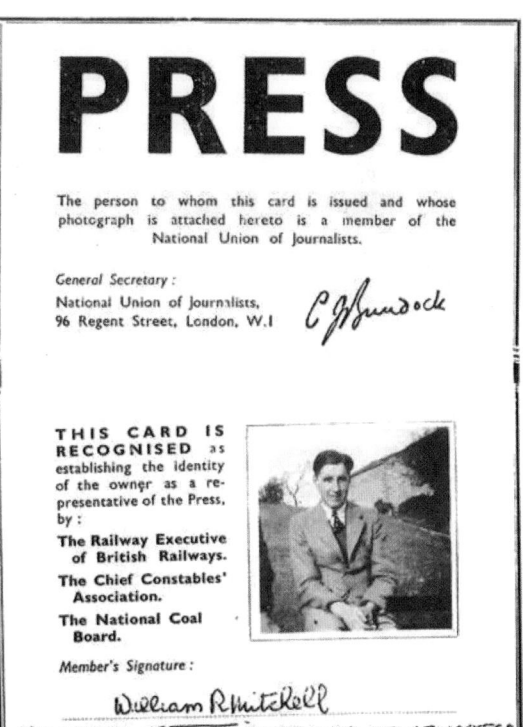

the following week. Again, we dumped the paper. The day came when a parcel arrived in the office. It was the type of parcel that the business manager got from farmer friends up the Dales he assisted with their tax returns. The manager pounced on the parcel, then binned it with revulsion. It contained the body of an albino carrion crow, attended by an army of red mites.

On hearing of a notable death, the 'black book' was consulted. It contained cuttings of biographical interest. These were presented in the past tense and a catch-line added, 'More to come' (which in due course was the report of the funeral). This catch-line was not removed, as it should have been, in the obituary of a prominent millowner. Readers were informed he was survived by a wife and daughter. Tongues wagged when they saw the errant catch-line 'More to come'.

Typographical errors were common which meant that wedding reports could be unintentionally entertaining. A bride who wore a string of pearls was reportedly wearing 'a string of pears'.

Journalism turned out to be a laugh a minute.

A Dales Editor

Dad was to write a piece many years later about a future editor, Jack Heald. When he attended Jack's funeral in 2014, he marvelled at the use of The Dam Busters Theme for one of the hymns!

For thirteen years, the *Craven Herald* has been edited by Jack Heald, who was born and bred in Skipton, domiciled in West Craven for many years and invited to return to Skipton and occupy the Editor's chair following the tragic death, in a caving accident, of the young and talented Ian Plant. That was in March 1980.

For Jack, Ian's death was a great personal loss. It so happened that his tenancy began on the first day of April. He adds, disarmingly, 'a lot of people think there is some significance in the date'.

He took over a paper being printed on a machine bought second-hand from the *Yorkshire Post* in 1936. I remember it well.

It was about as sophisticated as Grandma's mangle. If anyone read the small-type newspaper conscientiously their eyes were soon prickling with fatigue. Estate agents were complaining that their lovely photographs were reduced to 'black blobs'. A reader could scarcely tell whether a property for sale was a baronial hall or a back-to-back house.

The appeal of the *Herald* remained through the generations and so did the make-up. As Jack Heald says, 'If you look at the issue when the newspaper became a weekly in 1873 and compare it with last Friday's issue, the only superficial difference will be that the white paper of 1873 has yellowed with age'. A transformation occurred four years ago, with its acquisition by the Westminster Press, one of the largest groups in the land.

The paper now has a high-tech genesis at Bradford. Jack, who has just retired as Editor, comments, 'Dalesfolk are conservative with a small c. They say, "Don't change the paper". Now, with a slightly smaller page size but many more pages, the little old ladies complain it's too heavy to lift!'

Jack's penship has taken in most kinds of writing from lively leaders to critical reviews of musical and dramatic productions which, in some cases, have stirred up as much passion off-stage as they did at the time of presentation. His forty years in journalism began with tapping out copy on an ancient typewriter and ended with him recording via a word processor. His early memories are of hot-metal printing. Towards the end of his career, and in the cool, almost clinical high-tech world of today, Jack found himself yearning for the old sounds and scents – the clatter of machines and the aroma of printer's ink.

A Yorkshire Grace

O Lord, who blest the loaves and fishes

Look down upon these twa wee dishes –

And tho' the tatties be but sma'

Lord mak them plenty for us a'

But if our stomachs they do fill

'Twill be another miracle.

Tales of a dryland sailor

Work at the Craven Herald was interrupted by two years of National Service in the Royal Navy. This was to have an influence on Dad throughout his life as he readily admitted returning to the disciplined and orderly life in the period following Freda's death. Little material is available from his service days but I did come across this piece relating to it after he died. An unfulfilled book idea?

In the 1940s, wearing a uniform of the Royal Navy, I went to sea – for just a few miles. I was on the ferry from Stranraer to Larne. I never lost sight of land. The sea was uneasy. One of the other ferryboats had sunk in wild weather. I exchanged glances with some old folk sitting opposite me. They were smiling at my efforts to persuade my stomach to cope with sea sickness.

As I crossed there was time to think of my naval career up to that point. When I was 'called up', I reported to a dryland 'ship' near Wetherby Racecourse. My first embarrassment was when, with a friend, I visited a touristy part of the River Wharfe. We hired a canoe, which capsized in mid-river. There was a mass chuckle from the holidaymakers as two sailors, dripping wet, waded from the water.

When I reported to HMS Royal Arthur at Skegness, I expected a fine warship to be at anchor just offshore. It turned out to be a former Butlin's holiday camp and my first

naval duty was to be on guard, baton in hand, at a set of toilets. Thence to Elgar country, where I joined others rowing a naval cutter on a lake in the shadow of the Malvern Hills. Being flat-calm, it could hardly simulate an ocean.

I 'passed out' (in an academic sense, not as a result of too much ale) and became a Supply Assistant – one of the lowest of the low – at the Royal Navy Air Station at Ford in Sussex. I was not at Ford for long. A signal came transferring me to RNAS Evanton, somewhere in Scotland. I tried to find the place on a map. I was on the south coast and my destination turned out to be a place of modest size beside the Cromarty Firth. Reaching it by rail was a prolonged operation. I decided to alight at Skipton for a short family visit. Mum met me and advised me to stay on the train, which I did. At Carlisle, I missed a direct connection to Inverness. It was Sunday morning and virtually everywhere was closed down.

In the navy

Crossing to Glasgow, I seemed to have the city to myself. Almost twelve hours passed before I caught the train that would take me to Evanton, known in naval terms as HMS Fieldfare.

The supply officer ran his home on naval lines. Daily orders – his, not the official ones – were pinned to one of the inner walls. The family might be gently rebuked for using too much coal. This officer had a fondness for the birds of wild places. So had I. We occasionally met while crawling through rush-beds down by the Firth. One day, in office time, he dashed out of his office, shouted my name and urged me to follow him. He pointed to a fly-past of wild geese.

Homely beginnings with the great Scotts

On his return from the navy, Dad joined Harry Scott at the Dalesman offices in Clapham. Scott provided the opportunity which sparked a long and illustrious career and gave Dad the single most important piece of advice he ever received, 'put people before things'. This article was written to mark Dad's fifty years with the magazine.

A letter from Harry Scott invited me to visit him at Clapham: 'There are a number of possibilities we might then talk over.'

An orange-sided Pennine bus delivered me, via Buckhaw Brow. The welcoming party was a hungry swan which should have been admiring its reflection while cruising on Ingleborough Lake. Instead, it found easy pickings in the village and amused itself by terrorising old ladies.

In those pre-bypass days all traffic came through the village. There were several blind corners and a hump-backed bridge. A large vehicle with a cargo of tinned food, then subject to rationing, had failed to negotiate the New Inn corner and descended into the beck, just below the big waterfall. What had for centuries been a quiet, law-abiding community became one of wreckers. Every house, even that of the constable who was in bed with sciatica, had its share of booty. There was one snag. The water had washed away the labels. No one could be quite sure, when they prepared a meal, what would feature in the main course. Sometimes it was fruit.

A short walk took me to t'Brokken Bridge where I was greeted by a dipper, a podgy dark bird with a white 'bib' which was doing its press-ups on a water-washed stone. The home of the Scotts, and *The Yorkshire Dalesman*, proved to be a double-fronted house, its façade covered by Virginia creeper; the main path consisting of blue-grey flagstones and its garden containing sheep-nibbled plants of various kinds. The Scotts took up residency in 1935, the removal charge from Headingley being seven guineas.

I was welcomed into a central passage, flanked by a squat table which I later discovered consisted of packets containing the latest issue of the magazine. Mrs Scott had covered the unsightly stack with a cloth on which stood a vase of flowers. Any visitors were invited to share in an unusual domestic industry which involved slipping copies of the magazine into 9in x 6in envelopes and then sticking on stamps before they were taken to Mr Brown at the post office.

Harry Scott called the largest downstairs room his office, whereas to Dorothy Scott it was a lounge, on temporary loan to the magazine. There was an intermediary room with one of the sit-up-and-beg style telephones on a table at which the Scott family breakfasted and where the morning mail was opened amid tea, toast and marmalade.

Imagine, if you will, an extremely large desk occupying at least half the floor space and walls lagged with books. There were scores of files and dozens of heaps of letters, plus a shoe box which would be Exhibit A in any *Dalesman* library, holding all the relevant documents for the first few months of the magazine's existence.

Harry Scott sat at the large desk, with his back to the coke stove. He regulated the heat using a piece of thick cardboard which was slid along the back of the seat as a baffle if the rising temperature threatened to melt his spine. My desk was in the darkest corner. A single electric light bulb protruded from a fitment on the wall, a piece of bent tin directing light downwards and providing a substitute for sunlight.

My first job of the day was to type on to adhesive labels a hundred names from the telephone directory. These were attached to envelopes containing sample copies, added to the stock hand-written by Dorothy Scott the previous evening and laboriously transported to the post office. It was reckoned in those days that anyone who had a telephone could afford to become a subscriber to what was then Yorkshire's only magazine.

There was one typewriter, which I used. A small portable, not used for years, was Exhibit B in the *Dalesman* collection. Harry had used it in his freelance days. He called it a 'tripewriter' because, as he said, 'nothing but tripe comes from a machine'. He used a pencil on copy paper which was cut from the damaged outer sheets of newsprint rolls delivered to the Craven Herald.

The circulation of what was known as *The Dalesman* rose steadily and with it the need for more staff and accommodation. This was met by some shrewd purchases, firstly of a range of old workshops from Ingleborough Estate and then two-thirds of the vicarage garden plus half the large barn which had been used in

Harry Scott

Victorian times to house the vicar's horse and carriage.

Back at Fellside, Dorothy Scott regained possession of her lounge. On a subsequent visit I was able to walk across the room without scraping my shins on wooden desks or running the risk of being smothered by an avalanche of books and files.

Beside the Seaside

There is the old tale of a Dales male voice choir which competed yearly at Blackpool, and made the occasion a full day's outing. Arriving by the sea, they enjoyed a paddle. This was the routine for several years, and then one year it was noticed that one of the baritones had very black legs. He was chaffed. 'By gum, Ted, thi' legs is mucky!' Ted replied, 'Well, yer mun remember, a cudn't cum last year!'

People Before Things

Old Mick the bull walloper

Yorkshire folk are the best in the world for a 'lie down and a meal'. This is the opinion of sixty-eight-year-old Michael Raynard, who lives in a small cottage in Chapel Street, Settle. He has enjoyed their company for half a century in almost every dale in the county but he is sufficiently well-travelled to be able to make a fair comparison. He has experienced their hospitality and the real judge of hospitality is he who has slept under the stars, as Michael has. He knows of their generosity; he is aware of their reputation for being 'tight wi' their brass'. And yet Michael is not a Yorkshireman.

Michael does not forget his first days of residence in the North Craven town some thirty years ago. He slept on the town hall steps! Do not think that these hard but free lodgings were not appreciated for since his youth in Carlisle Michael has led a nomadic life and he is well accustomed to the rigours which go with it.

Who is Michael Raynard? Settle folk and his many friends throughout the Dales have good reason to ask, for it is probable that only a few people could identify him by any other than the name which has established him in their affections. It is 'Old Mick, the bull walloper', a title which he himself helps to keep alive, a homely title which has readily appealed to Northern folk.

Old Mick's bull-walloping days have ended, however, and as he plods along the roadways at Settle he carries a privet stick which he first cut about five years ago. The real emblem of his cattle-driving days – a hazel switch with its strong powers of persuasion when in the right hands – he no longer uses.

When I first saw Mick he was walking down the road in the centre of the town. It was Tuesday, market day, and the weathered stonework of the Shambles looked down upon laden stalls clustering the market place and upon the dalesfolk who thronged them. It is appropriate that a first meeting with old Mick should be on Market Day for he has been associated with Settle Market for twenty-seven years, during which time he has helped with the erection of the stalls. He can recall the time just after the First World War when the market was coming into its own and when he used to stand with cattle in the open street, working with Irish dealers. There was no auction mart at Settle so he used to take the cattle into the country. If there was no sale there, he would drive them to Bentham, often in the middle of the night, or Kirkby Lonsdale.

Somehow, when I first saw him, I did not feel I should ask if the tall figure walking down the busy roadway was Old Mick for there was something about him that was distinctive. Instead, I followed him into a local hostelry and hung around as he discussed Brussels sprouts plants with a friend. The speed with which he later dealt with a pint of beer left no doubt as to his identity and a friendly 'How-do, Mick' from another man passing by came in the nature of an anti-climax.

Why is Old Mick's beer drinking a key to his identity? While serving with the army during the First World War, he received an injury from a bayonet which called for an operation and now he can drink twelve pints to twelve strokes of the clock with ease. He has been a big drinker all his life. His father drank a fortune, he told me, but he 'found it out' and began to preach temperance. Old Mick has spent too much on beer, on his own admission, but he is sure it does him good. But, as a navvy once said to him, 'In pub, spent sub.

Below and facing page: Old Mick

and spent it with good cheer; now I'm going down the road, saying d--- and b---- the beer.'

Old Mick has few rationing difficulties, for when he drinks tea he uses neither milk nor sugar, merely adding a 'pinch' of pepper 'to give it a bit of a kick'.

It is inevitable that Old Mick, because of his great wanderings, should have accumulated a large store of anecdotes. He told me of a strange experience he had some years ago. He was travelling from Skipton to Pateley Bridge late one evening and went into an old quarry. Discovering a cabin, the door of which had been blown open by the wind, he decided on sleep and settled down on some brace on the floor. About the middle of the night something came into the hut.

'I just said, "shoo" to it.' Old Mick told me, 'but it started sniffing over me, I jumped up and thought the Devil had come for me but it was only an old donkey that had come in. I had taken its bed.'

Old Mick was once working near Aberdeen with a little Irishman called Paddy Green but they decided to return to England and tramped down to Carlisle. Their money was spent, however, so they pushed on to Lancashire by way of Kendal. Eventually, they reached Liverpool and, seeking rest, they visited the docks and found shelter – in a huge water pipe, one of a number piled on one of the quays.

'Paddy got into one end of a pipe and I got into the other,' said Old Mick, 'but although Paddy took his shoes off, I decided to leave mine on. In the morning, we felt a jerk and found that a crane was lifting the pipe on to a ship. The pipe tilted and we both fell out into the water and were rescued by dock labourers, who took us to a workhouse. We dried our things before moving on to Chester.'

Old Mick recalled that the nastiest insult of his life was experienced while he was at Fewston. A fox terrier came out of the house and bit him.

'I told the woman who owned it, "Your little dog bit me, missus," and she said, "'I'll wash its mouth out when I've got time".'

The passage of the years has wrinkled Old Mick's skin but it has not taken the youthful sparkle from his blue eyes. It has certainly not blunted his memory and he remembered that the summer of 1921 was unusually hot. Or was it a story he told me that aided his recollection?

'Old Jack would never wash himself,' he said, 'and during that hot summer we were walking by the side of Semerwater. I says to Jack, "when are you going to wash yourself?" Jack, who was as black as a sweep, replied, "I don't know". As we were walking, I suddenly tipped him into the lake and told him he was not coming out until he had washed himself. A woman had given him a blue suit and he never wore a suit and after he had washed himself a bit and crawled out, I made him put it on.'

Old Mick has been as far away from Settle as any man. He has visited Tasmania, spent three years with the army in India, served in France and Belgium during the First World War and in South Africa during the Boer War. He has also been on extensive sea journeys on merchantmen. He has been into most counties in England, and knows Scotland and Wales well.

'If I were young again, I wouldn't stop here five minutes,' he said. 'I would be off to San Francisco.'

He has good neighbours in Settle and never runs short of anything but he is essentially a nomad and I would not be surprised to learn of him setting off one fine day down the road leading to – who knows where.

Annie Mason

AM: We always washed on a Monday. A woman from the village came in and washed. She was the chief person. My mother would be cooking. We could sit down perhaps ten of us and we always had a cooked meal.

WRM: What was the washday routine?

AM: Well, you started and you

had a dolly stick and you washed the best things first: pillow cases and sheets and tablecloths. You see, we always had a tablecloth even for the men. My father used to say, 'I won't sit down without a tablecloth and I won't ask anybody else to.'

WRM: What was used? I mean, that was the day before soap powders, wasn't it?

AM: Yes, well we had Borax, Borax was the first. You bought them by the half dozen wrapped up in a big sort of brown paper container.

WRM: Did you use carbolic soap?

AM: Yes, not a great deal but we always used Lever's. My mother used to buy it by the box. I don't know how many dozen there would be: long bars...

WRM: Of soap?

AM: Yes, long bars of white Sunlight soap. We used to have a traveller. Well, he was a local man actually, from Askrigg, and he was a friend of my mother's and he was a traveller for Lever Brothers in Liverpool. We always got soap and all kinds of things came from them. And we used to cut up this soap, take it out of the boxes and out of the wrappers and you cut it up and we put it in the bathroom cupboard to dry. I still do this, I always have.

WRM: Why is that, so that it will last longer?

AM: Oh yes, it dries and lasts longer. If I buy from Boots I always do that. I always take it out of its wrapper and dry it out for a couple of months.

WRM: And then, of course, on a lovely March day with the breeze blowing it must have been nice to hear the washing slapping on the line?

AM: Oh yes, you see we had a biggish paddock in which the lines were out.

WRM: What did you use for an iron?

AM: Well, we used to use a box iron, you know, with the heaters? And we also had a charcoal iron. I had it to this day until I got a man to clean out my outbuilding and I've lost it. It had a chimney on and I would think it was quite a relic now. We used to heat the bit of charcoal in the fire and then put it inside and then blow the bellows until you got the fire going. It was a marvellous contraption.

WRM: It hadn't been a good washday unless everybody was absolutely jiggered by the end of it!

AM: Yes, that's right!

Dalesfolk I remember: Bill Alderson

He lived at Angram, in Upper Swaledale, and was generally known as Big Bill. He stood over six feet in height. A nickname was bestowed on many dalesfolk so they might distinguish between the many members of comparatively few families. He was also referred to as 'Bill up t' Steps'. He told me, with a chuckle, that he had received one or two letters addressed to 'Bill up t' Steps, Yorkshire, England'.

At the age of five, Bill was enrolled at Keld School which was one and a half miles from home. When he was quite young he took field paths, stopping at various barns to fodder the cattle. His father went on the rounds later to 'muck oout' and water the stock. At the age of nine, Bill was taught how to milk a cow. He never, in a long farming life, milked using a machine. In haytime, he was mowing with a scythe at the age of ten. A long-bladed scythe was used. Hay was taken to the wintering sheep by creel, this being a wicker framework strapped to a man's back. An alternative to transporting hay was in sacks that were suspended from a sure-footed Dales pony.

Children took their midday meals to school. These improved at pig-killing time when you might have 'sausage and 'crappins'. Referring to his later life, Bill said, 'Belly keeps t' back up, you can't work without some packing'. As a schoolboy he made some pocket money catching rabbits. In the summer holidays he helped on the grouse moors and spent some time at dusty peat workings. Dried turves were eventually sledded down to Angram to provide a store of fuel. On a winter evening, the womenfolk assembled in a room heated by a peat fire and spent hours talking and quilting.

When his school days were over, Bill helped his father on the farm and raised money doing jobs for other folk. He walled, drained and spread muck. 'You could get plenty of work. Trouble was you couldn't get enough brass for it.' Bill recalled a continuous tending of sheep, especially at lambing time and in summer, on the days when sheep were washed in a dammed-up beck before being clipped. Men stationed themselves in the pools, ruffling the wool of sheep

Bill Alderson

that were thrown to them by their neighbours.

I had some happy times at Bill's home. As we discussed t' auld days, beside a roaring fire in a fine old dales farmhouse, Bill's wife provided us with light refreshments. I recorded some of the talk on tape, one winter's day placing the recorder too near the fire with the result that when I removed it it was almost too hot to hold. Thankfully, there remained on the tape some splendid recollections of Dales life in the past.

Dalesfolk I remember: Kit Calvert

My first chat with Kit Calvert, half a century ago, was on the bridge spanning Duerley Beck, which was milk-white in its progress down a rock staircase from the fells. Kit, the best-known man in Hawes, removed his battered trilby to reveal grizzle-grey hair that had not been disciplined by a comb. He rekindled his clay pipe with black twist and told me he had tracked down some good 'clays' in Northern Ireland. His ragged dog, knowing Kit's propensity for talk, settled down for a nap. In those days, traffic was at ten-minute intervals and, in any case, there would be plenty of time to get out of the way.

Kit pointed to the beckside building where Edward Chapman set up a creamery in 1896, using milk produced on the local farms. When trade slumped in the post-Great War depression, and the closure of the creamery seemed imminent, local farmers found a new champion in Kit. He became managing director of a new company which had a capital of £1,085. In the early days, Kit could not afford to be ill. He had to turn up on site each morning to tell the workmen what to do.

Kit loved to talk about the old-style farmhouse Wensleydale cheese.

'It more or less melted in the mouth and had a nutty flavour that came from the high moisture content. There was nothing like a good summer-made white Wensleydale. It was one of the casualties of the Second World War. High-moisture cheese didn't fit in with the Ministry of Food's rationing scheme.'

Only six farmhouse cheesemakers were left in the dale in 1945.

To Kit's regret it was commercially expedient to change from the cheese's traditional linen bandage and use a polythene wrapping. He introduced the Baby Wensleydale, a one-pound cheese that the average housewife might buy weekly. On one of his rare trips from the Dales, he attended a glittering assembly in Leeds where Wensleydale cheese was being

Kit Calvert

Collecting milk near Hawes

promoted and began his speech with the words, 'I'se nobbut a moorbird.'

He retired in 1967 when he was sixty-five years old, reputedly with at least half a million pounds in the bank. Wensleydale cheese is still a noted product of Hawes. Every 'round pound' that leaves the creamery bears a portrait of Kit, complete with trilby and clay pipe.

Kit Calvert's name survives as that of a bookshop, which is the successor to one he started in 1940 in main street premises he rented from a local solicitor. One of the first incidents he recalled was howling at his father and demanding, of all things, a Collins dictionary, price one shilling. The howling of the precocious nine-year-old brought results. Father, though a struggling quarryman, bought the book. Kit became a book collector when he acquired a copy of Edmund Bogg's Eden Vale to the Plains of York.

'Bogg often came to Hawes,' Kit told me, 'cycling up the dale with a pack of books on his back. He hoped to sell them to the local folk.'

Kit paid next to nothing for his copy of the rare and handsome *Ogilby's Book of Roads* (1698). He bought it at a farm sale.

'I'd to buy six hundredweights of books to get this… I didn't bother to bring the others away.'

If there was no one in attendance at the bookshop, a purchaser left any monies in a chapel collection plate. The first honesty box had an anti-theft device. It was nailed to a table.

Kit was a Congregational lay preacher who, according to the local poet F A Carter, 'preaches on t'ferst day o't'week / An' practices on awt' others.' During the Second World War he kept a Swaledale chapel open almost single-handedly, motoring over Buttertubs Pass in all weathers. Kit translated passages of the Bible into the dialect of his native dale so that Jesus, while walking 'by t'tarnside' and seeing the disciples fishing shouted, 'Copt owt?' To which they replied, 'Nowt.' Jesus advised them 'to cast thi net on t'other side o't'boat'. A friend said, 'It's unseemly.' Kit replied, 'Christ spoke in a dialect.'

When Kit died in 1984, the coffin was borne to its last resting place in Hawes cemetery on a cart drawn by Dolly, his favourite pony. Dolly belonged to his daughter. When she next went riding, Dolly insisted on taking the road to the cemetery. The gate being open, the pony entered and stood near the grave of Thomas Christopher Calvert, who to one and all throughout the northern Dales was known simply as Kit.

Hannah's Christmas

Hannah Hauxwell achieved national fame through television. There was an astonishing response from viewers when Yorkshire Television presented a Dales documentary, Too Long a Winter. Later she was invited to attend a Woman of the Year luncheon in London, which she enjoyed, and television cameras followed her around for another documentary. Fame came to her nine years ago. Television focused attention on her long, gruelling struggle against the land and the climate.

Hannah is now enduring her fiftieth winter at Low Birk Hatt, in Baldersdale. She was borne from a nearby farm as a small child. Baldersdale unfolds, endlessly it seems, to the west of Romaldwick, beginning in the temperate zone of Teesdale and ending in the shadow of lean Pennine ridges which, at Christmas, usually have a crust of snow and ice. Hannah has never liked winter and often dreams about what she imagines the Mediterranean to be like – blue sky, blue sea – as the gales pound her house, loosening yet more slates, and snowdrifts arch themselves against the buildings.

No one called last Christmas Day although there was a visitor on Boxing Day. Hannah has a supply of electricity but last winter the power failed for several days. The cold seeped through every stone of her house. Her trusty army greatcoat, of 1939 vintage, insulated her from the sub-zero temperatures outside. Within the house she swaddled herself in clothes, as well as blankets, when she went to bed. She recalls that one of the items she spread over her was a tweed coat that had belonged to an uncle. On each day without power she had but one meal. It was a cold drink and some corned beef, with a cold drink before bed at night. It was not that she was without food but the effort of coping with the cattle in grim weather left her little energy to care for herself. She could not light coal fires because the chimneys were in need of attention. Her only form of lighting was a stable lamp.

One of the memorable sights was when she became aware that the power had been restored by the valiant men of the electricity authority. Hannah had been clearing out the byres. She was moving manure to a heap in the gloom when she saw a blaze of light from a farm up the hillside. She went into her house and switched on the supply. A layer of ice in the electric kettle delayed her preparing hot tea. She had first to warm water in a pan to thaw out the ice. Slowly, heat returned to the rooms and made life within them bearable.

'I'm not really a Christmassy person now,' says Hannah, whose clear, rosy complexion speaks of days spent in the open air. Even on Christmas Day, she is absorbed by 'beast work'. As she reflects on the colder end of the year, she observes wistfully, 'I wish it was always summer.'

Hannah Hauxwell

Life and times of Tot Lord

Fresh-faced and breezy: that was Tot Lord of Settle – greengrocer, archaeologist, wildfowler and much else. Tot's glowing personality was the aspect you noticed first. Seeing that round, ruddy face, the floppy hat and tweedy clothes – with plus-fours, of course – you had a feeling that he had spent almost all his life on the moors. His countryman status was confirmed when you noticed his stick, tipped with a thistle-stubbler, a useful implement for stirring up a mole heap that might contain flints.

Although Tot bought and ran a greengrocer's shop in Cheapside he was never very fond of shop work, though he was ready to help out when necessary. He did not like the idea of working regular hours. His home was a short distance away up Constitution Hill at Town Head. It was a large Victorian house with spacious grounds. To walk up the drive was to enter an area that might almost have been a set for a Somerset Maugham story – dense shrubbery, an old palm tree, the glass-and-iron verandah. Beneath the verandah was a wicker chair, a table and the skull of an elephant.

If Tot was not otherwise engaged he would invite the visitor to see round his museum, occupying a large ground floor room. First, I would watch the ritual of unlocking the door then I had a glorious insight into pre-historic life through the skull of a great cave bear, a reverse barbed harpoon fashioned from antler, dragonesque brooches and much else. Though a private concern, it was one of the country's most important collections of objects from pre-history. Half the room contained show cases made by Tot himself.

Tot's fascination with pre-history was fuelled in 1924 when Dr Arthur Raistrick conducted a series of lectures in Settle on local history. When they were not 'in the field' Tot and friends met at the Pig Yard Club, a name taken from the building – one up, one down – in the yard owned by Tot's family. The talk was spontaneous, all-embracing, sometimes argumentative, always interesting. Raistrick recalls a small room with an old coke stove.

The most famous 'bone cave' in the district, Victoria Cave, had been extensively excavated. Its mouth was now a yawning hole on the scars. Yet in 1925 the members of the Pig Yard Club found a stalagmite floor in the extension of the cave and from beneath the

Tot Lord

floor came the remains of Ice Age mammals. Tot's finds included the remains of hippopotamus, the extinct narrow-nosed rhinoceros, extinct straight-tusked elephant, giant deer, spotted hyena and brown bear. They roamed the Dales when the climate was warm 120,000 years ago.

Tot Lord was an individualist. Who but Tot would have taken to a week-long excavation on Malham Moor a marquee and a bed with a brass head? Who but Tot would have installed a stove in the rock shelter known as Sewell's Cave? When working on Sunday, he welcomed his wife as she arrived with the ingredients of a good lunch. It was cooked to a turn and complete with Yorkshire pudding.

A restless man, he was forever striding across the hills, questing for the remains of early people. One pothole near Stockdale Farm was named after him: Lord's Hole. He ordered his life according to the seasons, being particularly active in winter, at dawn and dusk when the waterfowl were flighting. He spent many a summer's evening by the Ribble with rod and line.

To one of his fellow wildfowlers, EH Partridge, the brightness of Tot's face was distinctive: 'a red face which in the fading light had the dull glow of old baked brick.' One evening by the Ribble, Tot had related that he bagged a goose on the previous evening.

'At least I think it were a goose,' he added. 'It were a big white bird and I could hear it coming for long enough before I saw it.' To Partridge it seemed tactless to point out that no wild goose likely to be encountered in this country was ever white, 'but one could only envy him a dish that graced the more plenteously furnished boards of our ancestors,' It was, indeed, a thirty-two pound whooper swan which graced the pantry shelf for many days. Partridge was to recall the evening when Tot fished with a gun. He suddenly swung his firearm and discharged a barrel at the astonished man's legs as Partridge waded in the shallows, his mind intent on birds.

'The water was cut to foam behind me, and as I turned to ask him what the game was, I was cut short by a peremptory, "Look sharp! There's your ruddy breakfast!"'

Partridge turned to see a fine grayling, of about one and a half pounds, floating by, belly upwards. Tot, in reply to the other man's wonderment that he should have fired directly at him, said, 'You're wearing gum-boots aren't you?'

Much later, Partridge, who was a distinguished headmaster of Giggleswick School, was with Tot and his son Thomas. They crouched near the river, waiting for wild birds.

'It was not till we were sitting some fifty yards or so apart and surrounded by darkness that the full humour of the situation dawned on me. We were a representative company; a parent, an old boy, a day boy and the headmaster. And if the pupil was playing truant from prep, the headmaster was pretty certainly poaching. And I laughed till I could hardly shoot as I thought of the long spoon a man needs who would sup with the Devil. But we got nine mallard, two wigeon and a teal.'

Tot Tommy

Tot Tommy, a Metcalfe from Keld, ran the Midnight Express over Buttertubs to Hawes. This mini-freight service was used by the dalesfolk. A farmer might, for example, ask him to take a pair of clogs to Hawes to be repaired and Tommy would charge 2d for taking them and perhaps a penny for bringing them back. The name Midnight Express was a reference to the slow gait of his horse. 'You could hardly tell if he was stopped or going.' Tommy did some unsociable hours. He might set off from Hawes after dark and protect himself from the wild weather on Buttertubs by thick clothes, a cap and mittens.

Tommy Moore: the complete dalesman

Tommy Moore has been hand-milking cows all his working life. Nowadays, there is greater emphasis on hygiene. I smiled at the recollection of a friend who worked at an old time creamery at Dent where his boss, cheerfully ignoring the extraneous material which managed to get through, would say, 'Milk tastes o'nowt until t'cow has its foot in t'bucket.' Tommy remarked, 'If you did that today, they'd be soon after you at t' dairy.'

Two hazards at milking time are the proneness of a cow to kick over the bucket used for the milk and the cow-pat process that begins when the animal lifts its tail. The hand-milker turns his cap so that the neb is at the back and presses his head into the flank of the cow as his fingers rhythmically massage the teats and bring forth spurts of milk that make a distinctive sound on the sides of the pail.

'It's a knack. When you start, hand-milking is hard work.'

In winter, illumination was provided by a candle stuck on a window-ledge. The kits of milk were wheeled in a barrow the hundred and fifty yards to the old dairy beside the beck.

Tommy's hand-milking career began with gentle Shorthorns, which were allowed to retain their horns. This was the type of animal they had to find when they began to film the adventures of James Herriot in a Dales setting. Tommy says, 'There were no Friesians and no tractors then.' At haytime he was 'scrattin' wi' horses and hand-rakes. We mowed all t'wallsides wi' scythes. It was a matter of getting every bit you could.'

Tommy has a stock of Friesians today. The buildings are connected to the national electricity grid and the milk is conveyed to a tank for collection by a vehicle from Hawes Creamery, so the milk from Tommy's cattle makes a small but important contribution to the production of Wensleydale cheese.

The memories of a half-forgotten Dales life spilled out of Tommy's mind. We grimaced at the thought of muck-spreading by hand-loading a horse-drawn cart with muck at the midden and distributing it in neat little heaps from which it was 'scaled' or spread with the help of a fork. 'It was a back-breaking job.'

Haymaking

Sally's parrot

Her real name was Sarah but she was Sally to the folk of Giggleswick. In the early 1930s she was living at 'top house on't flagstones' just round the corner from Cravendale, the home of Dr Charles William Buck. Sally had been housekeeper to his brother, Richard, a dapper man with a small beard who lived in retirement in Craven Terrace in Settle.

Sally's claim to notoriety was as the owner of Susie, a blue-crested parrot, which in 1932 was reputedly fifty-seven years old. On sunny days she moved its cage out of doors, where local lads encouraged it, without success, to memorise swear words. Susie smoked a pipe, did simple sums, helped herself to drinks using a small wooden goblet and could imitate the walk of a drunken man. The talented parrot would, on command, blow a trumpet and salute pictures of the Royal Family. Not a feather moved when she was shown a picture of the Kaiser. Sally displayed her at local events and garden parties in the Dales. The money earned went to charity.

It was almost certainly Susie who was kidnapped by Dr Buck and, wait for it, Edward Elgar who, as a young man, visited Giggleswick by train, changing at Leeds. Buck's daughter, Monica, told me of the day when her father and Elgar kidnapped a parrot and, with the bird settled in a cage suspended from a pole, they bore it shoulder-height towards Settle. While crossing the bridge, the bottom of the cage fell out and a bemused parrot found itself displaced. Whether or not it swore was not recorded.

The writer of a newspaper article in 1932 ended with the words, 'A cow bell tinkled in Giggleswick's quaint little street before I left. I looked back. From the shoulder of the grey-haired old lady in the cottage Susie was roguishly shaking a bell, anxious for me to turn so that I should see her blow me a kiss.'

At a Dales dance

'I'd like to do this old-fashioned waltz but I daren't reverse.'

'Why, would it make you dizzy?'

'No, but it would unscrew my wooden leg.'

Far from the Madding Crowd

Sad day as bus company completes its final journey

The last Pennine bus, in its familiar orange and black livery, will run tomorrow. The company was founded in 1925 and says it cannot continue in the face of increased competition. It was founded by two Skipton brothers, Arthur and Vic Simpson. Having served in the Great War,

they took up engineering. Their lives changed significantly when they visited Leyland Motors in Lancashire for three Overland buses. Arthur selected the bright

A trio of Wensleydale bus staff

colour scheme, seen on a bus parked in the yard and used by the works football team.

Details of the new service, along with a timetable, were published in the *Craven Herald*. The name 'Pennine' was seen as robust and related to 'the backbone of England', in part of which the service would operate.

The bus had fourteen wooden seats covered with oilcloth. Petrol was supplied in drums. A bus used six gallons a day, at a cost of seven and a half pence a gallon. When Pennine began to use a manually-operated pump, fuelling a bus was a weary process.

Where should the service start? The driver parked outside Dobson's in Skipton High Street. The only passengers on the first run were Bertha McKell, a schoolteacher living in Gargrave who taught at Coniston Cold, and two children. An anxious parent saw them on to the bus near Long Preston and they disembarked beside the Maypole Inn in the village after travelling about half a mile. Stretches of the main road between Skipton and Settle were narrow, strewn with loose stone and having flanking dykes for much of the way. With no official bus stops, the driver pulled up beside any person who looked interested. The fare from Skipton to Gargrave was five pence (single) and eight pence (return).

The service became very popular and, on occasion, the bus would creak with a full load of passengers. Some bravely stood on the running boards or leaned over the bonnet. One dark Saturday night, a policeman boarded at Long Preston and had to stand in a crush of passengers as more than forty competed for fourteen seats. Some passengers, unseen by the policeman, had been on the running boards. When the bus stopped, they appeared in the darkness to pay their fares. The policeman, keen to know how they had travelled, was told by the quick-witted driver, 'They haven't been riding, they've bin running at t' back.'

It was not unknown for a farmer on his way to market to deposit a calf, swathed in sacking, at the back of the bus. A sheep in transit was seen tethered to a back seat. Parcels of all shapes and sizes would be carried. The firm would, as they say, carry owt! Fish and chips were ordered by villagers who met the nine o'clock bus out of Skipton. On reaching Settle, the driver would collect them, piping hot with plenty of packing, from the shop in the Shambles. The orders were distributed on the return journey.

When I joined *The Dalesman* in Clapham I used the service regularly and heard many

Arthur Simpson, *founder of
Pennine Bus Company*

fascinating tales from the staff, particularly the amiable inspector Harold Dryden. He told me of a farmer who was keen to get home for milking-time. He asked the driver, Lionel Thornton, if he could improve his performance.
It was the type of bus on which the steering wheel could be lifted free by just removing a nut. Lionel did just that. Handing the steering wheel to the farmer, he said, 'If you can do any better, have a go.'

At a time when the Pennine buses laboured up Buckhaw Brow on their way from Settle to Ingleton, it was such a popular run on a sunny Sunday that a

Mr Robinson set up a stall by the head of the Brow and sold fruit, vegetables and rabbits.

When I think of Pennine, innumerable tales come to mind. There was the day when I was travelling from Clapham to Skipton and a goat was among the passengers. I heard the story of an old lady who boarded the bus creakily, bought a ticket for Skipton and asked the man at the wheel to drive carefully. She was going to hospital. As she left the bus in town, the driver asked her how she felt. 'I'm all right,' was the reply, 'I've got a jelly in this bag and it hadn't quite set when I left home.'

A postman's life

I once asked John Cunliffe about his most famous creation, Postman Pat. The character was devised as a dalesman, operating from the fictitious hamlet of Greendale. The success of the programme raised the profile of the rural postmen and their red vans are a familiar sight around the Dales. Yet when I began my Dales wanderings, they usually either walked or travelled by bike.

Tommy Brown, of Gunnerside,

delivered letters to forty-five lonely farms in Swaledale in all weathers over as many years. It took him six hours to cover a round of from twelve to fifteen miles.

Jack Rukin, of Keld, covered Tan Hill Inn on his round. He was the only regular contact the residents had with the outside world.

Fred Falshaw, a postman in upper Wharfedale, told me at one point he had to ford the river. If there was a spate, he would attach any mail to

A country postman

a stone and hurl it across. One day, he reached the riverbank to find the farmer waiting for him on the other side. Fred attached a postcard to a stone. The stone fell at the farmer's feet but the postcard, becoming detached, fell in the river and was swept away. Said the farmer, 'Nivver mind, Fred, tell me what were on 't.'

The Dales postman assumed heroic proportions in times of heavy snow, notably during the late winter and early spring of 1947. On Malham Moor, the postmen took it in turns, day by day, to walk the four miles from Langcliffe to the farmsteads. Edith Carr recalls that the mail was frequently left at her home, Capon Hall, to await collection by neighbouring farmers. When a postman entered the kitchen in the early afternoon, he was a sorry sight. His outer clothes would be stiff with the cold and his eyebrows and hair covered with rime.

Mr Chaffers, short and stout, was determined that thick snow would not stop His Majesty's mail from getting through. He arrived at the farm with great ceremony, puffing and blowing. He would then unpeel his waterproof leggings and the brown paper and newspaper he had wrapped round his legs, securing the wrappings with thick, coarse string. He had great faith in his 'thermal' wear and trundled for miles looking for all the world like a well-wrapped parcel.

Postbox at Yockenthwaite

A taste of some old-fashioned medicine

Yorkshire Air Ambulance has given the term 'first aid' an exciting new meaning. Expertly piloted and with trained paramedics on board, the yellow 'whirlybird' is a familiar sight in emergency situations throughout the county.

In Grandfather's day, doctors were well-spaced in the Dales. In one remote tract of dale-country, a farmer remarked to a visitor, 'We dee naturally up here.'

Medicine was stuff you got in bottles, shaken before use. Pills tended to leave a nasty taste in the mouth. The doctor asked a farmer's wife if her husband was taking his pills religiously. 'Nay. He curses every time I give 'im one.'

A charge was made for medical services. In the 1930s, a Settle doctor with two surgeries a day, six days a week, charged 3s for a consultation, 7s for a bottle of medicine and 3s 6d if called out to the home of a sufferer.

Dr Will Pickles took over a practice at Aysgarth in Wensleydale on the death of his partner in 1934. Will, a homely chap, reckoned there was hardly a man, woman or child living between Bainbridge and Wensleydale of whom he did not know the Christian name. He could also name most of the dogs and some of the cats. He would visit remote farms on horseback and perform emergency operations on kitchen tables, by candle or lamplight.

Dr Edgar of Settle, whose practice took in the scattered farms and broad acres of Malham Moor, employed a man named Tomlinson to drive his horse-drawn trap and open and close the dozens of gates set across the road to a place like Darnbrook. At night, when the only light came from carriage lamps, Tomlinson left the trap now and again to check that he was on the desired route. The doctor needed a coachman to attend to the restless horse when he arrived at some remote house or barn.

Dr Jane O' Connor, with a practice in North Ribblesdale, was fond of recalling when she opened a gate to a hill farm. Two opportunist tups, tethered to each other at their horns, rushed through the gap into the next field. In their hasty progress, they knocked over the doctor and brushed against her car. On her next visit to the farm, when expressing surprise at sight of very early lambs, the farmer reminded her of the tups and said of the lambs, 'They are early – thanks to you.'

Many of the old-time doctors of the Dales were local heroes. They did their best, often in grim circumstances of terrain and weather. Fred Lawson, the Wensleydale artist, said of Will Pickles, his great friend, 'He stops and chats and gives confidence. That's what a lot of these old people want. You'd be surprised how much medicine ends up down the sink.'

A Dales tailor

After an evening meal at a Dales farm, I watched the farmer don a smart black jacket and sit beside the kitchen fire. He was being thrifty rather than ostentatious, determined to wear out his wedding suit which he had bought some forty years before. Dalesfolk are dress-conscious when the need arises, such as for a funeral when they require some 'good setting-off clothes'.

A couple in Upper Wharfedale phoned a relative in Settle to say that they might be calling at the outfitter's before long because a close friend was ailing and might not last long. They had 'nowt good to wear'. When they did not call for a while, an explanation was demanded. The reply was, 'He got better.'

These two stories come to mind when I think of Henry 'Cos' Cosgrove who allied himself with John Reeson, an outfitter in Skipton, and spent more than thirty years visiting customers all over the Dales. Cos had a Morris Minor. For a year, he was shown the rounds, including the direct route between Malham and Bordley which Mr Reeson managed quite well on foot. It was somewhat demanding when he chose the same route for the car.

'We went in the car the way he went because it was the only way he knew.'

Happily, in especially dry conditions, the link with Bordley was made.

Cos started work on his own account in March 1947 when the Dales held the cores of drifts from one of the worst winters ever. He reached Rainscar, back o' Penyghent, to be told, 'You've done well. The postman hasn't been yet.' Another time his car foundered in snow and he had to be dug out by four men, each with a shovel.

'When I started I knew nothing about farming but I soon discovered that farmers wanted to talk about nothing else so I soon picked it up.'

At one farm he was taken out and shown a flock of sheep which was having a difficult lambing time.

'All the farmer wanted was someone to talk to. He wanted comforting.'

Conversely, there were times when the outfitter wanted comfort, such as when the customer complained that 'trousers aren't reight. There's one leg shorter than t'other.' He was correct. The kitchen floor across which he walked was sloping.

At Darnbrook on Malham Moor were Mr and Mrs Robinson and four lads, the tallest of which stood at six feet one inch.

'Mother ordered a suit from time to time for one of the boys or her husband, generally because a suit had gone damp with mildew while hanging upstairs in the days before electricity. They did not wear the cloth out.'

Cos took his first order for a suit for one of the lads and had it made up.

'It turned out that I'd looked at the measurements in Mr Reeson's book and got the wrong set. I made it for the smallest but Peter was the tallest. He came down with his sleeves half way up his arms and his trousers at half-mast. I quickly offered to make another.'

The Dales farm kitchen Cos entered on his rounds was spartan by modern standards, with flagged floor, pegged rug before the fire, wooden furniture. There might be a clothes horse with a blanket draped over to cheat the draught from the door.

'The farmers' wives liked me to give them pattern books when they were out of date. The samples usually finished up in a pegged rug.'

Dalesfolk were good payers but inclined to settle up when they got money, such as from the sale of lambs.

'At one call,' said Cos, 'I knew that if the farmer went into the house I might get paid. We would be talking and have a pot of tea. He had a rota system and if your name came up you got paid. If not, you waited until next time. Suddenly, he would reach for a cardboard box and then I definitely knew that some cash would be forthcoming.'

Heard in Co-op

'She's miserable as sin. Never speaks to anybody. And when she does speak – she says nowt.'

Broadcasting in the Broad Acres

In 1958, the BBC broadcast from Alum Pot, that huge limestone shaft above Selside. T'wireless lads, who arrived in a Land Rover and two cars, were greeted by members of the Bradford Pothole Club. A considerable length of cable was laid in Long Churn, the approach passage, and into Alum Pot itself. Aerials set up on the moor allowed interviews to be transmitted to the village, then passed forward by landline.

Nowadays, you may chat to almost anyone, anywhere, via a pocketable device. Sound and vision bombard our senses. In the 1930s, a hush descended on Skipton as Joe Wilkinson made his wireless debut by singing When I Married Amelia. That tinny voice had novelty value. It's not the case today. I recall visiting a farmstead where the farmer had dressed for a special occasion. He would sit before the radio and listen to Saturday Night Theatre.

For a host of families living at villages and farmsteads well away from electricity supplies there was a broad smile when George Newsholme, of Clapham, appeared. In 1952, he invited me to join him in his little blue van on one of his rounds when he would exchange batteries. He kept wireless voices and music strong and clear. At one spot he showed me a battery he had just collected from under a milk stand. A piece of black cotton had been tied to it. Said George, 'The folk here are good payers but they like to be certain they've got a new battery and not an old one.'

During the colder months thousands of people switched on their radio sets to have their hearts warmed by a programme called The Northcountryman. This was a weekly miscellany about northern life and people. It was introduced by Philip Robinson, whom I met at Clapham. When he left the village I noticed he had some catkins pinned to his overcoat and there was the strain of a folk tune on his lips.

A major source of memories of t'owd radio days was James R Gregson, a Yorkshireman who had many ups and downs in life as a lift attendant. He was born in Brighouse in 1889. I had my first long conversation with him in 1956 at Riverside Cottage, near Linton-in-Craven. His first broadcast – a fifteen-minute talk about theatre work – was in 1924. He recalled, 'The studio was like a padded cell. The microphones were of the 'carbon' type. When they became tired and faint, the engineer would kick them about the studio to shake them up.' Producers had to 'twiddle their own knobs'. This task was later left to the engineers.

Bertha Lonsdale is another name one associates with the early years of radio. She contributed some memorable plays, based on factual events, to the BBC's Children's Hour, transmitted from Manchester. I remember her radio portrait of Lady Anne Clifford, who has strong connections with Skipton Castle. The names of her castles were recited as though they were in a litany.

The BBC recording unit occasionally turned up at Clapham, where *The Dalesman* was published. They had a large car to which extra strong springs had been fitted to accommodate the mass of equipment that was on the back seat. I have occasionally appeared on television, most recently near the old single-span bridge at Clapham where, in times past, the radio has simply recorded what was said. Now it was being televised as I chatted with Matt Baker for the Countryfile programme.

Bill chats to Matt Baker on BBC Countryfile

Tales about babyhood

In the Dales, there was a joke about everything, even babies. When a farming couple were rearing their first child, the wife went upstairs. Her husband, standing by the cot, was looking at it hard and long. Touched by the sight, her eyes filling with tears, she put her arms round him and said, 'Nah then, Jack, what are you thinking about?' He replied, 'Nay lass. I think we paid too much for yon cot.'

Norah Johnson, who became a District Nurse, and also trained as a midwife, told me of 'rare trips' through a snowscape to remote farmsteads. A career that was largely to be spent in the Craven Dales started in Upper Teesdale. When Norah was summoned, in snowtime, to a birth at a farmstead on the Strathmore estate at Holwick, she had to leave her car at the roadside, trudge through snow and cross a beck to reach the remote building. Twins were delivered. As Norah was about to leave, the farmer brought her a horse to ride. He remarked, 'When tha reaches thi car, just turn t' hoss round. It knows it's way 'ome!'

A baby born at a Stainforth farm was recorded as BBA – baby born on arrival. Norah found it lying on the bed. It was a third child and had come quickly with no complications. The farmer had done what was necessary.

The father of six children waited patiently for the schooldays to pass and rejoiced as yet another child left school and became a full-time worker. When the last of the six was freed from what he was inclined to think of as 't'shackles of eddication', a friend asked, 'how does ta feel now tha's gitten all t' pullets laying?'

A farmer's wife, having visited a neighbouring farm to see the new baby (usually referred to as 'it') said, 'It's such a big lad: it bawls like a calf.'

Holidays

An old man from Hawes paid his first visit to London. He was watching traffic outside the Mansion house when a policeman remarked, 'Busy, isn't it?'

'Aye, there's a trip in frae Hawes.'

Traditions

Showtime at Muker

The steward at Muker Show, in upper Swaledale, advanced on me with a broad smile and outstretched hand. I expected a handclap and, instead, received a blow from a rubber stamp. The steward collected £1 and I entered the Showfield. On my hand, in purple letters, was stamped the name MUKER, proof that I had paid for admission. A farmer said, 'Thoo wants to be thankful we didn't use a hornburn or clip a bit of ear out!'

When I drove into a field set aside as a car park, only one other vehicle was in sight. Soon, the dale road was busy with Land Rovers towing trailers as farmers conveyed the best of their sheep to the showground. The ancestors of those sheep, plus cattle and horse, had to walk.

I was attending the 87th Grand Annual Show of the Swaledale Open Agricultural and Horticultural Society (pause for breath!). The farmers were too busy for much conversation. I watched a man attaching labels to tufts of wool on the backs of his sheep. 'Do they stay on?' I inquired. A minute or two passed and he replied, simply, 'Some on 'em do'. Muker Show may be a relatively small event but its sheep classes are renowned as befits a parish at the heart of the Swaledale sheep country.

A man who was 'fluffing up' wool on the fleece of a sheep, wool that had doubtless been crushed in transit, explained this 'titivating' operation as being 'like a woman does afore she goes out anywhere. She wants to look pretty'. There was much plucking of hair from the fleece and legs.

If the judges were overawed by the presence of some of the keenest flockmasters in the north they did not show it. They took in the general characteristics of the sheep and then moved closer, parting the wool, testing its quality and looking for 'black bits'.

Ewes suffered a total loss of dignity when they were turned on their backs, then reared into a sitting position, where their bellies sagged. The teats were examined. 'A judge wants to see if t'tits is

Sheep at Muker Show

reight,' said a friendly farmer at my right elbow. 'Some tits can be duds. An t'yow must 'ave suckled lambs.'

The sheep enjoyed a brief spell of liberty when released into a smaller pen. Two tups met each other head to head though without serious intent to maim as they might at tupping time, later in the autumn. The judges studied each sheep's carriage. Then the owners were allowed to recapture them, jamming the sheep in a corner and then grabbing the down-curved horns. Nature might have had hill farmers in mind when the ponderous horns were developed.

The judges looked grave. They briefly deliberated, peered at the sheep, made an odd sortie to check on some minor detail. A few minutes ticked by before the red, blue and yellow rosettes were distributed to the Swaledale tee-ups and yows, superstars of Muker Show. I asked my farmer friend if he agreed with the judges. 'They're not far oot,' was his response.

By 12:25pm, judges of classes in the marquee had reached their decisions and the canvas doors were thrown back to admit the public. The show catalogue included a note, 'Luncheons for all officials at 12:30pm.' Each diner settled down to a sumptuous meal.

We then wandered back on to the field.

In the produce tent, Mr Willcock, of Hurworth, risked a hernia as he lifted a huge parsnip, guessing its length at over three feet and its weight at perhaps seven pounds. Rows of carved sticks and shepherds' crooks reflected the ingenuity and skill of humble craftsmen who had plucked sticks from hedgerows in autumn, tracked down the horns of aged tups and fashioned them into objects that were both useful and decorative. In their hands, horns had taken on the forms of woodpeckers, foxes and hounds. My favourite was one on which the shaft swelled out naturally into a shape that a nimble mind and fingers had converted into the head of a horse.

Mrs Harker, who lives twixt Langthwaite and Low Row, had come with Wensleydale-type cheeses, made in a Swaledale farmhouse. She has a background firmly established in the life of the upper Dales. On the field, children ran races and young folk tried their hand at reversing a tractor and trailer along a constricted course. The welly-throwers limbered up. One spent five minutes ramming the sides into the foot of the welly, which he threw with such force that the object nearly went into orbit. 'Screwed-up wellies' were pronounced illegal. Many a welly went off course. Said the good-natured announcer of one wild throw, 'That'll have taken the top off someone's ice-cream.'

Back at the sheep pens, farmers discussed the finer points. The supreme champion was as last year, a majestic tup kept by Joe Hall who keeps 1,200 Swaledales near Bowes. It was the only sheep he showed this time.

The fell race was longer than usual as the river could not be crossed from stone to stone. A torrent of peaty brown water prevented it and the bridge had to be used. A farmer who was leaving the field summed up the feelings of most when he said of the show, 'It's bin aw reet…'

Old Age

An old lady in a retirement home decided to make life more interesting by stripping off and streaking through the lounge. As she passed through the hall, two short-sighted men looked on.

'Was that Betty?' said one.

'Nay, I don't know – but whoever it was her dress needs ironing.'

Dancing in the Dales

In this merry month of May, four dances will take place at Tosside, between Ribblesdale and Bowland.

'It's an amazing place, is Tosside,' one of the regulars told me. 'It's out on a bloomin' hilltop, miles from anywhere, yet t'dances allus go off well.'

A dance was cancelled last winter because all but the main road lay under snow. There was no space to park cars. Another time, when a band from the upper Dales could not negotiate a way through roads plated with snow and ice, someone brought along some 'canned' music. Dales dancers are a tough breed. An old couple related to me, quite calmly, how they drove home from Dent on a snowy road that had shrunk to the width of the council's plough.

The old hut at Tosside which once served as an institute was heated by a central stove which invariably glowed white-hot. When the moment came for the band to strike up, two burly men slid metal rods into slots on either side and carried it outside where it thawed any lying snow. Chat with the old folk of the upper Dales and you hear that people danced wherever there was room – where they would not become 'leg-locked'. At Muker, dances took place in a room near the Farmer's Arms. It was an upper floor, flavoured by the smell of horses that were stabled underneath.

For an authentic barn dance held at Douk Ghyll in Craven a cart cover was stretched across the barn doors to cut down the draught. Harry Wilson and two companions from Settle were paid ten shillings for an event which began at eight o'clock in the evening and ended at four the following morning, with an interval for supper. Kit Craven's Band, also from North Craven, used a handcart to transport a piano to the villages.

Those dances at Muker attracted lads from a wide area. They demanded value for money.

'If a dance didn't go on till two, we wouldn't go to it. It didn't matter what time I got home as long as I got into t' house afore my parents got up. I've seen me take my shoes off so that my dad wouldn't hear me goin' to my room.'

Attending farmers' dances at Bentham, one son cycled ten miles, danced until two, then cycled home. For the Primrose

League Annual Ball, this same youth caught the last train to Bentham, danced until three or four in the morning, found shelter to play cards with friends and caught the first train home.

Dales dances are often slow to warm up. There is chatter among old friends – just a few at first. The dance tends to become crowded a little just before supper. This may be a cup of tea, a couple of sandwiches and a bun but a 'special do' might have a buffet where so much good food has been assembled that the trestle tables groan. I once had my tea poured from a can that was dipped in a bucket. There's almost certainly an EEC regulation to prohibit that sort of thing today.

No one wastes much time drinking and eating. The catering organisation is slick. You know when supper is imminent when a 'Friendly Waltz' is played. As the last strains die away, doors and hatches are open, women appear with trays or tables holding plates of food and in minutes everyone has a sandwich clenched in their teeth. One band included a pianist, though the instrument was sluggish. Too many cups of tea had slithered into the open top. After the break at Austwick one night, my wife and I were once caught having two minutes' rest. We were approached by an old-timer who said, 'Thou wants to git up an' shak thi supper down.'

When they get going there is a jauntiness about Dales dancing. In an old-tyme waltz, an old farmer said to his partner, 'Eh luv, can you reverse?' She replied, 'Are you gettin' dizzy?' He said, 'Nay – but you're unscrewing my wooden leg.'

Dancing at a Dales hall provides escapism and exercise for those who have not been imprinted by television and who still enjoy setting out to have a good time. The old tunes are the best. There is something of the flavour of music hall, the 1914–18 war and the inter-war period. Among the 'Top of the Dales Pops' are 'I Do Like to be Beside the Seaside' and 'Down at the Old Bull and Bush'. Most of the music is unashamedly sentimental.

I like my dancing well-organised so that after a few twirls I can resort to automatic pilot and concentrate on talking to my partner. Gossip is the small change of Dales life. A Doris Waltz is just the thing. There's nothing simpler. In a Progressive Barn Dance you find yourself dancing with the long and the short and the tall, from gangling schoolgirls and young ladies wearing next to nowt to old 'uns who were waltzing and fox-trotting before you were born. Sometimes you bruise your fingers on whalebone corsets.

There will be many reasons why people go dancing. It was an old chap in Wensleydale who remarked to me, 'If I didn't git up an' dance, I'd lock up wi' arthritis!' As another enthusiastic owd-time dancer once said, 'It's t'best way of shortening the winter.'

Last of the 'terrible' knitters

The drummy sound of clogs against cobbles in the main street of Dent drew attention to Betty Hartley, clad in Victorian garb, who was knitting on her way to visit her good friend Elizabeth Middleton. The two ladies carry on the tradition of the 'terrible knitters 'e Dent.'

Hand-knitting as a means of eking out a pittance earned in farming was practised in several Yorkshire dales, from Dentdale to Swaledale, and in some of the Westmorland dales as well. Robert Southey, in a miscellany called The Doctor, used the memorable expression 'terrible knitters 'e Dent'. He recounted in dialect the adventures of Betty and Sally Yewdale. As children, in around 1760, they were sent from Langdale to Dentdale to be taught how to knit. Betty was 'between sebben an' eight year auld, an' Sally twea year younger'. The word 'terrible' in this context does not mean 'shoddy' but 'great'.

However, saying that, the two girls were soon wearied of excessive knitting and, after several adventures, returned home to a tearful reunion with their parents.

Almost ceaseless knitting was not an amusing diversion. It was hard work. Originally, the Dent spinners spun and used local wool. When there was not enough to go round, a weekly delivery of wool was made by cart from Kendal – it began at the end of the eighteenth century and lasted for about ninety years. There was an urge to knit stockings, jerseys, mittens and gloves to supplement a miserable income on the little upland farms. The same cart would take finished products back to Kendal, among them stockings and gloves.

The coarsely spun wool was known as 'bump', and a bump-knitter rocked backwards and forwards as her nimble fingers handled the four curved metal needles. One needle was slipped into a hole at the end of a dagger-like knitting stick which was held firmly by a leather belt.

The Dent knitting stick is a collectable antique. Many were made locally, some for young men who were courting. A suitor handed his stick to a lady-love as a love token, or maybe to hint at what was expected of her when they were married and needed to earn a living.

Betty Hartley's grand progress up the cobbled street at Dent was staged for a television film, though she and Miss Middleton gave numerous demonstrations of the craft. They sang the old Dent songs as they plied the needles. This tradition had developed to stimulate the knitters to maximum efforts. Betty Yewdale recalled a particular song in which the knitters called out the names of dalesfolk as they got to the end of every needle,

Sally an' I, Sally an' I
For a good pudding pye,
Taa hoaf wheat, an tudder hoaf rye,
Sally an' I, for a good pudding pye.

Sally and Betty Yewdale got round the problem of not knowing many by using the names of folk back in Langdale. The two girls sang the song, altering the names at every needle, 'and when we com at t'end cried "off" an' began again an' sea we strave on o't'day through.'

I recalled that I first saw Betty Hartley and Elizabeth Middleton when the Settle-Carlisle Railway centenary was being celebrated in 1976. A special train drew up alongside the 'down' platform at Dent, the highest mainline station in Britain. Theoretically it was spring but rain was being hurled

Dent knitting

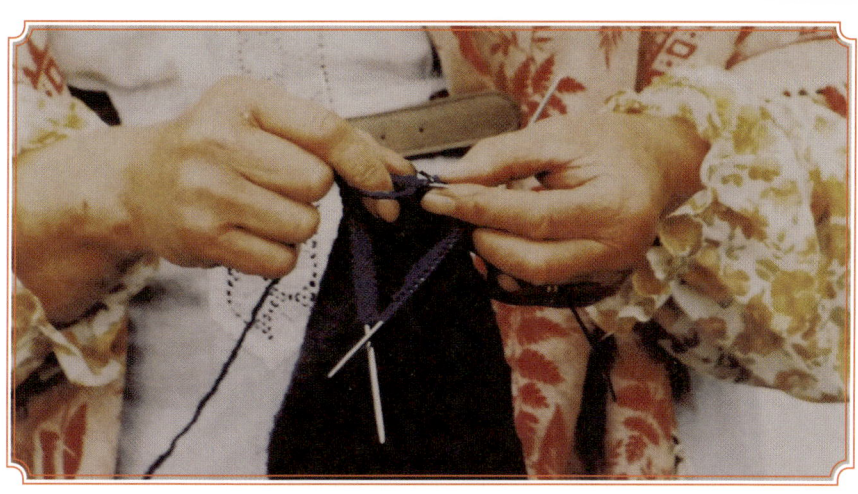

at us by a wind full of spite. Ice cream was on offer. There were few takers. The 'hand-knitters' stood out because each had donned a lace-fringed cap, long gown and fancy shawl.

I asked Betty when she had first knitted in the special Dent way. Her mother had taught her when she was three years old. She has a stick which was made by William Oversby, her grandfather. At one time, she said, virtually everyone in the dale knitted. Her grandfather had done this while sitting at the front of a horse-drawn cart on the way to Dent station to collect a load of coal.

There was something satisfying in being allowed to handle a knitting stick which had been used for many years. It was shaped like the wing of a goose. A ledge along the widest part prevents the stick from slipping behind the leather belt which held it against a knitter's body.

The two ladies use Arran wool which is 'as near as we can get to the original type. In the old days, the wool was thick and oily, dirty and rather smelly. A lot of stockings were made for use with seamen's boots. Lots were exported to Russia.' In the heyday of Dales hand-knitting, a pair of stockings was knitted for a shilling.

Dales tales of a Christmas past

One of Settle's old-time fairs was for the sale of geese. Birds raised at the farms, having walked through pools of tar to reinforce their webbed feet against the rough surface of the roads were driven into town. A good goose could be bought for £1. It was said that only the quack was wasted. Grease kept in jars became an embrocation when the children had bad chests. The wings were kept for spring-cleaning – nowt like a goose wing for removing cobwebs.

The Giggleswick and Settle Brass Band used to make rounds of the farms, at each of which there was usually some punch to taste. One bandsman received so much drink he poured some into an instrument and sipped it while walking between farms. When the band toured the immediate area, the elderly members were given the task of knocking on local doors and taking a collection. One by one, they hobbled off home, staggering a little from the liquid hospitality provided. The inebriated 'knockers' were replaced by other band members until there were few left to play.

Christmas at the big houses was a happy time for the family but a period of unremitting work for the domestic staff. Ivy Segger told me of working for a lady with social pretensions. She was only eighteen but expected to work from six in the morning until ten at night for ten shillings a week.

'If I was up and about after ten she would find me another job. I slept in the attic. There was a tiny bit o' carpet at the side of the bed. It was bitterly cold in winter.'

At Christmas this lady entertained two local families who arrived grandly by car. Mr Peacock was a solicitor and Mr Partridge the head of Giggleswick School.

'I had to cook the meal,' said Ivy, 'which started off with homemade vegetable soup that contained owt and

everything. Then we had turkey and the usual trimmings, followed by a sweet.'

The staff's food consisted of, 'whatever came out of the dining room. Take it or leave it.'

In contrast, the McEvoys of Stackhouse were well-disposed

Cartoon Christmas card from Old Amos illustrator Rowland Lindup showing Bill and colleague David Joy

towards their staff. Far from living off the scraps, the staff had among other edibles a huge piece of sirloin.

'At Christmas everyone was agog,' I was told by Alice Maunders. 'The children cut little pictures out of magazines to make parcels. In the kitchen, cook and I were busy with the plum pudding and the mince pies. Cook always made some rhubarb wine.'

On Christmas Eve, the staff gave each other presents. 'I remember going up to the top bedroom where I slept,' continued Alice. 'On the bed was a little parcel, the first Christmas present I had ever had.' It was a magazine and a bar of chocolate, tied together with a piece of ribbon. It had come from Mrs Armistead, the children's nurse.

Churchgoing was a feature of Christmas morning.

'Afterwards, Mr McEvoy said that he would like all the staff to come into the billiards room. We stood in a line and entered, one by one, in order of merit – Mr Johnson the butler, then the housekeeper and head housemaid, the children's nurse and then the cook. Then it was me, who was just learning to be a cook. We received our presents and Christmas good wishes.'

In the evening, the staff walked into Settle to listen to the band playing and dance in the market place.

At a farm on Malham Moor, Edith Carr and her family had a huge Christmas tree in the corner of her living room.

'It was the time before fairy lights. Candles were put in little metal folders that were clipped on to the branches. As I went out to milk the cows, I said to the rest, "Don't touch the Christmas tree. And under no account light the candles till I come back".

'Having milked the cows I took two big jugs in to the kitchen table. We always used a lot of milk. I went back into the shippon. I had not been there long when one of the children came out shouting that the Christmas tree was on fire. I immediately thought, "What if the house is burnt down, especially on Christmas Day?" I flew into the house. The children had lit the candles as soon as I had got out of the way. The dry branches of the tree got alight. One of the children had the presence of mind to go into the kitchen for something to put out the fire. The first thing she saw were the two jugs of milk.'

It was indeed a memorable Christmas for all the wrong reasons.

'Ours was a troubled household that Christmas Day. The following day, clearing up operations took place. The overall smell was terrible.'

First footing at White Scar

For fifteen years, I turned up bright and early on 1st January to 'let in the New Year' at White Scar Cave near Ingleton. We at *The Dalesman* had known Mabel Sharpe for years before I was invited to 'first foot'. She was superstitious, explaining that this was because she was the daughter of a seafarer. I did so more for the novelty of the occasion than because I felt my presence on New Year's Day would enhance the year's takings. I had, for good measure, to visit the paybox to wish the enterprise well. Mabel refused to let anyone enter the cave until I had been there. I was not expected to take anything symbolic, like a piece of coal, and there was no one to witness my embarrassment at talking to rock and wood. The routine was unvarying. I was greeted by Mabel and her cairn terrier. I received a torch and the key to the cave and was told to be sure and say a few encouraging words at the vital paybox. My first-footing took me on a traverse as far as the first waterfall. When I returned the key, I received a cup of coffee and a piece of Christmas cake.

Lecturer's magic lantern effect that brought nature to life

Frederic Riley's 'magic lantern' shows on nature and the Craven countryside lasted for half a century. The magic lantern effect was created by using a gas supply and a cylinder of oxygen. Riley told of cumbersome projectors. One projector of the time consisted of a biscuit tin enclosed in a wooden box and fitted with a row of acetylene burners. It caught fire and was carried from the room with a shovel.

Frederic usually asked for a pointer to indicate specific features of a picture. The offers ranged from billiard cues to a long-handled sweeping brush. Visiting a Craven school and finding his throat dry, he asked for a glass of water. A small boy handed him a jam jar with the explanation, 'I've taken t' minnows out.'

Recalling how his words and pictures were often applauded, I remember the time when I presented a slide show in a theatre often used by Frederic, at the Science and Art School at Skipton. My subject that evening was a tour of Yorkshire, including a study of the red roofs of Whitby. The projector had an extremely powerful bulb and the heat affected the emulsion of the film. Before my eyes, and those of the large audience, the red roofs of Whitby began to bubble. The applause I got was for the wrong reason.

I gave lots of slide show talks about the Dales. At Hellifield Methodist chapel, the projector failed after a few minutes. A voice from the adjacent kitchen sounded through a crowded hall, 'Nothing's broken. I'm just changing over t' plugs so we can have cups o' tea at half time.' At a Women's Institute, the old lady who offered to change the slides did so at random. One slide bobbed up three times.

Slide Shows

Chairperson asked to get 'a celebrated wit' for the next meeting. She had failed and so had arranged for the presence of two half-wits!

A chairlady said, 'I am deputising for Mrs Smith, who is on holiday in America. I am sure we all wish we could be with her.'

Yorkshire's Scenic Variety

White walls of Yorkshire

The owner of Grange Farm at Bempton was reported to be selling thirteen acres of 'rugged cliff face' and three acres of cliff-top land near Bridlington. He rightly described the property as a 'unique piece of land'. Here is the seaward termination of the ridge of chalk which extends across the Wolds to end abruptly with white cliffs up to four hundred feet in height. The chalk has an overlay of boulder clay and is thatched with grass and wild flowers in great profusion.

The waves break their backs against cliffs which are cracked and seamed, holding – in spring and summer – about a hundred thousand pairs of nesting seabirds. The musky smell of guano curls over the cliff. Indentations form echo-chambers for the growling guillemots and razorbills. The guillemots on their ledges look like rows of brown and white skittles. Kittiwakes, forming Europe's largest nesting colony, are everywhere. Excited birds swirl like snowflakes in a blizzard.

Flamborough Head, to the south of Bempton, has a North and

South Landing. In good weather, it is outrageously colourful, the sky and sea tones, plus the white and green of the cliffs, being diversified by the multi-colours of the cobles which lie on the shingle like seals that have hauled themselves out of the water to sunbathe.

The inshore fishermen had an arrangement whereby if weather conditions changed and the boats were diverted from the North to the South Landing on their return, the small son of one of them might have to leave school early to take the donkeys round to the South Landing, where they were needed to transport tackle and fish back to the village.

I voyaged in the coble Prosperity. The boat was coaxed from a shore which in places was covered with weed and elsewhere was pebbly. Thousands of pieces of chalk, torn from the native cliffs, had been wave-licked into smooth pebbles.

Sand martins twittered as they flew round their nesting holes, which they had drilled into the soft ground between the chalk and the grass. Kittiwakes rose from

the water to form white clouds. Far out, the sea was Prussian blue. Near the shore it had a turquoise hue.

The coble, with its sturdy construction (larch on oak) was exceptionally steady. I was told that long years ago cobles were built at Whitby by 'hand and eye'. If I took a line down the centre, the two halves would not match up precisely as they would in a modern coble.

We sailed on a high tide so we hugged the coast, first entering Thornwick Bay to the north. Here the Smugglers' Cave was so large it looked as if the cliff was yawning. As the voyage resumed, I watched the lines and chevrons of seabirds returning to the White Cliffs after feeding offshore. Puffins were working their wings so briskly that I entertained the thought that they might break off through bone-fatigue. The flight of gannets was languid and graceful. On my first visit to Bempton, no gannets were nesting there. Then some birds from Bass Rock began to occupy broad ledges which had been used by guillemots. Into being came the only nesting colony of gannets on the British mainland.

We turned south to enter a shallow inlet containing the pinnacle known as the Queen's Rock. Once there was a king. 'It's always said that the King Rock collapsed about the time that George VI died. It's probably not quite true…' The high cliffs were bird-busy. Guillemots adorned the ledges and stood on shelving rocks close to the sea. At our approach, the birds dived into the breaking waves and departed underwater. Kittiwakes shouted. Jackdaws chacked. Herring gulls gave laughing calls, as though responding to some doubtful jokes.

Our return to North Landing was escorted by more incoming seabirds. Ours being the last voyage of the day, the coble was hauled from the sea using wire rope and tractor power. The tractor pulled, the cable tightened and the coble ran smoothly on skids formed of baulks of timber deftly deposited before the advancing boat.

Along the cliffscape a myriad seabirds flew with sunlight upon them.

School

A teacher taking a class on a nature walk asked a farmer's son how many sheep he could count in a nearby pasture. He replied, with an air of pitying superiority, 'Them's noan sheep. Them's bluddy tups.'

Nineteen forty-seven

'When the snow falls dry, it means to lie…'

Such was the situation just sixty years ago when the first flurries of snow heralded a never-to-be-forgotten winter. It was a biting north-easterly wind, classified by dalesfolk as 'lazy' because of its inclination to go through rather than round all living things. Winter began with flurries in late January. From the first Sunday in February, the 'snow dogs' were howling. There were drifts up to fifteen feet high.

Snow covered much of England and Wales. The storms were especially severe in the Yorkshire Dales. Farmers who struggled on to the moors above Littondale and Embsay could hardly see over the drifts. Dalesfolk tuned their lives to continuing hard frost, the dispiriting moaning of the wind and an Arctic prospect. Snow was tinted red by a sun that set like a fireball. Not until the end of March did teams of men with shovels or bulldozers make the roads on Malham Moor, over a thousand feet above sea level, passable for traffic. As late as June, the cores of old snowdrifts might be found in shady places.

The wind made this winter memorable. It blew day and night, sweeping the high ground and dumping snow on road and farm track. A ganger on the Dent length of the Settle-Carlisle Railway recalled, 'Biggest part o't snow was on t' railway. There were next to nowt on t' fells.'

The line was kept open to Ribblehead, enabling a schoolteacher to travel to Horton-in-Ribblesdale on the footplate of a locomotive. In the village, she had a long walk between walls of compacted snow.

The wife of a railwayman at Salt Lake Cottages provided a footplate crew with food and drink. The grateful men gave her what they called 'black snow'. It turned out to be coal.

The line was impassable for eight weeks. At the southern end of Blea Moor, one of the new-fangled jet engines was set to work to clear a drift. A sceptical railwayman, sitting on a rail sucking at his pipe, said, 'Engine buzzed away for I don't know how long. It managed to clear a yard o' snow so they gave it up as a bad job.' All you could see of Dent station, where sleepers set on end were classified as a 'snow fence', was one big block of snow.

A railwayman who could not leave his home, each door being blocked by snowdrifts, cleared the pantry and cut his way to freedom, piling snow in the empty pantry. The stationmaster sealed off his home from sneaky draughts by spraying it with water from a hosepipe. The water froze instantly.

The loss of sheep was considerable. A North Craven farmer recalled, 'T'sheep were forivver bleating for a bit o' fodder.' Hundreds of chilled, hungry animals might perish on a single farm. Some sheep had the sanctuary of snow caves, away from the searching wind. An Airedale farmer saw a sheep struggle from a drift of snow with a dead sheep frozen to its fleece.

As the food stock at Capon Hall on Malham Moor dwindled, so did the cattle fodder in the barn. Edith Carr recalls that 'the cows were bawling all day. We could not feed them too much at a time. They were permanently hungry.'

The postmen took turns, day after day, to walk the four miles from Langcliffe, arriving at a farm with outer clothes stiff with the cold and eyebrows and hair covered with rime. Elsewhere, a man who had ordered a daily newspaper by post eventually received fifteen with his letters at one time. Dalesfolk shared what food they had. Because no milk could be moved from the area for several weeks, it was converted into butter and cheese.

Relief came to the remotest farms from the sky. At Halton Gill, Darnbrook, Capon Hall and others, the RAF, using Dakota aircraft, dropped bales of hay for their residents and their starving stock. One pilot was so precise in his haydrop at Garsdale a bale went through a farmhouse roof.

The Carrs at Capon Hall got advance notice about the air-drop when a postman said he had heard about it on the radio and that those affected should, if possible, make a prominent cross on the snow. They used provin' sacks and old motor oil to mark out a cross. The oil was set alight at the appointed time. The family, hearing the buzz of aircraft engines, watched the Dakota fly round the house once or twice before making a low approach – so low, indeed, that the farmer and his family could see the doors opening. The first drop was of parcels of food, then the planes returned to drop hay for the stock. This was in bales which burst on impact with the ground.

'We tussled and tussled for the rest of the day and just about all night to get most of the hay under cover,' recalls Edith Carr.

Clumps remaining on the snowy field were greedily consumed by sheep.

There was a day at Capon Hall when Robert and Edith Carr stood in the chilly silence of the yard. Then their faces lit up. Across the moor came the bubbling call of a curlew, a harbinger of the spring.

Many years later, Edith was travelling by bus from Settle to Skipton. A woman joined the bus at Gargrave and sat beside her. They chatted about Malham Moor and the 1947 winter. Edith mentioned the help afforded by the RAF. Her new friend had helped to pack food that was dropped from the Dakota aircraft to the desperate dalesfolk and their snowbound stock.

Tour brings thoughts of the past

The Tour de France revealed the grandeur of the Dales as never before. I think especially of the sunlit views in a spectacular route taken by hundreds of cyclists as they crossed our district. The massed competitors, crowds of spectators and views of glorious landscapes were transmitted to millions via film shot from a number of helicopters. I was thrilled to be able to peer down on a host of familiar features. I remember in particular glancing at the rooftops of Skipton Castle in its glorious setting. Sunlight and clear air had ensured that we would see the landscape at its best.

Along the roadside, spectators were sitting on bales of straw. I was amused when two great-grandchildren, having excitedly watch the Tour pass through Skipton, spent the following few hours cycling in the family garden.

Cycling through the Dales was a novelty in 1882. Cyclists were uncommon and, when seen, were objects of awe and wonder. Herbert Waddington recorded an old-time cycling run from Skipton to Malham. When three cyclists left the city of Leeds early one August morning their object was to discover the source of the River Aire. Mechanically, they had graduated from cycles with iron-rimmed wooden wheels ('boneshakers') to solid rubber tyres.

The trio pedalled via a bustling Skipton, the state of disorder being derived from the fact that the annual agricultural show had been held the previous day.

The cyclists left the main road at Gargrave and, pausing for a short time at Kirkby Malham, looked in the church for curiosities, one of which was the signature of Oliver Cromwell.

The old-time tour took in a view of Gordale Scar. Returning to Malhamdale, they spent a little time at Janet's Foss, saw the infant Aire, had cups of tea in a garden near Malham Bridge, then returned to Leeds by the same route. They had travelled seventy-eight miles.

Rough-riding cyclists stormed the Three Peaks – Ingleborough, Whernside and Penyghent – on 1st October 1961. It was the first annual Three Peaks Cyclo Cross, one lap of twenty-five miles. It was organised by the Bradford Racing Cycling Club. Two members, Harry Bond and John Rawnsley, went over the course in May, completing it in 3 hours 54 minutes. In the 1970s, John, a prime cyclist who became a great friend of mine, completed the Pennine Way, Britain's longest continuous footpath, in less than three days.

Back in the 1880s, a West Yorkshire lad who propelled himself to school on a penny-farthing bicycle had to cover about two miles from his home. For two years he welcomed this alternative to walking. His velocipede, a three-quarter-size bicycle, had been handed down in the family. There was no one to take it on so it was sold for ten shillings.

Halliwell Sutcliffe, novelist with a fondness for the Yorkshire Dales, moved to a fine house at Linton-in-Craven in 1907. To Sutcliffe, the dale country was steeped in romance. When he was not tending his rock garden, he donned Norfolk jacket and breeches for an excursion on foot or bicycle into the remote corners of the Promised Landscape. He had no use for a car. A bike was fast enough. Such exercise kept him lean and wiry. At a funeral service in Burnsall Church, Alfred J Brown described Sutcliffe as a genuine dalesman. He numbered him among 'a very small number of scholar-gipsies who forsook the towns and gave himself, body and soul, to the peace of the hills'. Whenever he took his bicycle along moorland tracks, peace remained. There was no motor to rouse the echoes or startle the grouse.

The Tour de France will remain in the memory of dalesfolk if only for the glorious, sunlit dale-country through which a mass of cyclists pedalled and for the televised views from the helicopters and roofs of buildings we normally only see in profile.

Shuttle service to the underworld

I first descended Gaping Ghyll in the 1950s with the Austwick Field Club, including the family of WK Mattinson, a man who as a small boy had stood at the rim of the pothole on an August day in 1895 when M. Martel, the French speleologist, became the first person to descend, using rope and rope ladder.

Now there's a shuttle service to the underworld. Since my last descent, a simple but effective numbering system had been introduced and I had to sign to exonerate the organisers in the event of injury or (let it be whispered) death. I borrowed a helmet and was allowed to root among a heap of old waterproof clothing in a small tent. It was rather like looking for a bargain at a rummage sale. Then I walked the plank on a gantry, took the seat, feeling like a customer of Sweeney Todd, the barber, as a lever was pulled to draw back the plank. The operator signalled to the man on the winch. I had a sudden sinking feeling…

With my elbows and legs well tucked in I passed within inches of the rock. The fluted limestone was adorned by ferns. So far, progress was slow. Then I entered the chamber itself, feeling like a spider dangling from its silken thread under the dome of St Paul's Cathedral. I was wet. The tumbling water was breaking into blobs all around me. Water pattered on my helmet and hit my waterproofs with a dull sound. Yet it was all over in a matter of seconds. Released from the chair, I was able to stand and let my eyes accustom themselves to the gloom of the massive chamber. Having already explored the galleries and fearing a sudden rush of begrimed and weary potholers which could create a queue to ascend my chair, I took the next available opportunity to return. Years ago, when a charge of ten bob was made, I was told it cost 'nowt' to descend. I was paying for the return journey.

Courting

A timid young man and his girl stood watching two cows rubbing their faces together. 'Tha knaws, lass, I could do that,' he said. She replied, 'I can't stop tha'. It's not my cow.'

Drystone walls add to Dales landscape

Walls made without a dab of mortar jostle round our Craven farmsteads and villages. They also pattern the fells. To visitors they are a source of wonder. An American visitor called them 'those cute stone fences'. Norman Nicholson, one of my favourite north-country poets, began one of his poems with the notion that the wall 'walks the fells'. It is a 'grey millipede on slow stone hooves'.

A drystone wall may look rigid but it gives. One of my old farming friends said, 'I've got a wall that shuffles. Then it gives.' It had become 'gapped' to use a local term.

There are various hues according to the geological setting. I enjoy seeing the pearl-grey of limestone walls at the head of Malhamdale. They are rarely just grey. Like the chameleon they

Drystone wallers in the Dales

respond tonally to conditions of light and weather. On a sunny spring day a limestone wall looks bone-white. As sunset approaches in thundery weather, they become pink or purple. When the fellside is snowy, there is a wall pattern in black.

The golden age of walling extended from about 1750 to 1840. That was the heyday of the Enclosure Awards. William Bray, an eighteenth-century traveller, wrote of pastures that had, in recent times, 'been lately divided by stone walls of about two yards high, one yard wide at the bottom, lessening to a foot at the top'. He calculated that a good waller might complete a stretch of about seven yards in a day.

Two Arncliffe brothers devoted themselves to wall-building on the 'tops' in the summer and to odd-jobbing in winter. When walling, they would leave home at seven in the morning, taking some food, usually a loaf and some onions. Two roods of wall might be built during a long summer's day (a rood measures between five and a half and eight yards).

In poor weather, a waller might be seen wearing an ex-army greatcoat or might have an old sack around his shoulders. Any waller who donned gloves or mittens was considered to be a cissy.

Among the old-time wallers was Dave Hannam who constructed the six-foot-high wall across the

top of Penyghent. In around 1860, according to local memory, he walked from his home in Horton to the top of Penyghent to do the work. For his effort he was paid half-a-crown for a rood of seven yards.

Among the interesting features of drystone walls is the 'cripple hole'. It allows the passage of sheep but not cows from one pasture to another. Mixed grazing was possible. Such a hole is built between two wallheads and a lintel, sometimes two lintels if a long stone could not be found. Old railway sleepers had been used for this purpose. When not in use, a cripple hole was covered by a piece of flagstone or a wooden pallet. Sometimes a spiky bush might be pushed into the gap.

My father-in-law, a West Craven farmer, was fond of telling the story of how a local waller became known as Moonlight Jack. He was a good waller who gave value for money. He ensured that there were good foundations, that the courses were level, joints were crossed, plenty of 'through stones' were used to bind the two sides of a wall together and the capstones fitted snugly. When he reached a stage where there were no gapped walls left, he would go out on a moonlit night and pull down a few stretches to keep himself in employment.

A corner of Yorkshire: Goathland

Goathland, in a green depression on the North York Moors, was in the 1950s so peaceful that half a dozen people was a crowd and Matilda, a Swaledale sheep, dropped her lambs in the shadow of the churchyard wall. Today, to a host of telly-viewers, it is Aidensfield, in Heartbeat country, a name relating to a popular television series of whodunnits. Goathland teems with happy fans. Television has frozen certain features as they were in the 1960s, when Nicholas Rhea based his Constable books on the place. Malcolm Mostyn's garage, with its blue-painted doors, is world-famous as the workplace of a fictitious character called Bernie Scripps who also runs a funeral service. A collection of 1960s cars are usually drawn up near the 1960s-style petrol pumps.

Ilkley Moor Baht 'at

The lad who courted Mary Jane on Ilkley Moor is nameless but most of the world knows about him through the somewhat grisly song which became a Yorkshire anthem. He went to Ilkla' Moor 'baht 'at' (without a hat) and ran the risk of catching his death o' cowd and being buried, to become food, in turn, for worms, ducks and humans. What started out as an example of bawdy West Riding humour can be sung lustily and easily at communal events, largely because of the catchy tune, originally a hymn tune called Cranbrook.

I wore a hat on Ilkley Moor (Yorkshiremen do not make the same daft mistake twice) but a gale-force wind lifted it, carrying it for a few hundred yards until it lodged against Millstone Grit, an outcropping lump of coarse brown rock which rose above the litter of last year's bracken crop. The wind that day was the grandfather of all

Cow and Calf rocks, Ilkley Moor

Pennine blasts. On the journey up from town to the Cow and Calf Rocks it not only rocked the car but produced a tuba-like solo by forcing itself through a fine crack between a side window and its frame.

Later, I leaned against the blast, baht 'at, but have lived to tell the tale of Ilkley Moor – a 1700-acre slab of rough, high land, sprouting heather, crowberry, bracken and bent. A few clumps of pines cling desperately to the ridges. There are boggy places where one might easily sink up to the knees in peat and sphagnum moss. Along the edges of the Moor are signs of man's activity in the little farmsteads. A flattened area near the Cow and Calf Rocks is intended for car parking. Until the 1939–45 war an eighteen-hole golf course was laid out near Panorama.

The demarcation between the moor and the town is sudden and, since cattle grids were fitted to the high roads, quite decisive. The moor sheep once found their richest grazings in local gardens, with a partiality for wallflowers. On a single disastrous night, sheep ate about £100 of prize carnations in a garden.

Ilkley Moor is not a precise enough term for those who have to administer it. In the byelaws the term 'the moor' means Ilkley Moor, Holling Hall Moor, Panorama Rocks, Heber's Ghyll and 'all waste and other land' described in the conveyance of 1893 from Marmaduke Francis Middleton to the Ilkley Local Board.

The Moor rises to an elevation of 1,320 feet. Pennine rain has formed watercourses in places like Spicey Gill and Willy Hall Spout. They replenish the Tarn which lies between Troutbeck Hotel and Craiglands – on which skating regularly took place during old-fashioned winters.

The fame of Ilkley Moor is not based solely on an old ballad which was composed impromptu during the visit of a West Riding choir and set to the familiar hymn tune. There are mysteriously carved stones, one carving having the shape of a swastika. Rediscovered in the 1870s, it is now protected by barbed wire and railings. There is a copy of it in the Manor House Museum in Ilkley. Scores of carved stones, some bearing 'cup and ring' symbols dating back thousands of years, have been recorded on the Yorkshire moors. Mid-Wharfedale is a particularly good place to see them. It is an eerie sensation to come across such markings, made by the first human occupants of the area, in this Yorkshire wilderness with its bold outcrops of millstone grit, its rustling bracken, ling and bogland.

A corner of Yorkshire: Janet's Foss

Stroll along the beckside path beside Malham Beck towards Gordale Scar and you will enter a tract of woodland carpeted by rocks, moss and ransoms (wild garlic). At Janet's Foss white water tumbles over a tufa screen. Foss is Norse for waterfall. The name Janet is said to be derived from Jennet, queen of the fairies. She lived in a shallow cave behind the fall and presumably wore something more practical than the customary ballet dress. Trolls, those nocturnal, dwarf-like creatures of Norse folklore, may have been homed here before tourism developed. The noisiest of the springtime denizens are rook squabbling over nesting rights. The plunge pool at Janet's Foss was an ideal washing place for sheep which were dipped and the wool ruffled by hand about a fortnight before clipping.

Janet's Foss, near Malham

History

Looking for Lady Anne

As a native of Skipton, I grew up hearing stories about Lady Anne Clifford, the first of them doubtless being related as I was pushed in a pram up 'the Bailey', a favourite local walk. I began to think of Anne Clifford as another aunt. It pleased me to learn this year that my grandson in Skipton had, with that limitless enthusiasm known to the young, rapidly become an expert on the Cliffords through a school project. He had some artwork represented at an exhibition in the parish church last January, when the birthday of Anne Clifford was celebrated.

I visited Skipton Castle anxious to learn a little more about Anne's early life. As I walked through the archway, I saw the cheerful Clifford flag was flying from the big round tower. Lady Anne's parents were George Clifford, the 3rd Earl of Cumberland, and Lady Margaret Russell, daughter of the Earl of Bedford. Their marriage had been arranged when George was seven and Margaret was five. Three children were born to them. There were two boys who died young and daughter Anne who was to become the indomitable Lady Anne who would live through the reigns of Elizabeth I, James I, Charles I, Cromwell and Charles II, dying at the age of eighty-six. Anne was born in the castle in 1590. I inquired about the precise chamber in which the birth took place. It lies in a part of the castle not open to the general public and which became associated by name with Mary Queen of Scots who had been put on trial and kept prisoner. The chamber was prepared and kept available in case the castle was needed to hold her but no record exists of her visiting Skipton.

Anne Clifford, being born at a time when infant mortality was high, was doubtless baptised at the earliest opportunity. That would be provided by the chapel within the walls of Skipton Castle. Everyone who visits Skipton Castle retains a strong mental picture of the Conduit Court, with its flanking buildings and a tall yew tree (which was planted by Lady Anne following the restoration of the castle after the Civil War). A stone surround encircles the base of the tree. Beside this lies what appears to be a stone basin. The significance of that basin has been realised. It is a font, almost certainly from the castle chapel (within which, during the Civil War, were housed the horses of Cromwellian cavalry). It is almost certain that this font was used at the baptism of Anne Clifford.

Lady Anne, taking over the family's northern estates at the age of sixty, promptly put into effect an extensive restoration scheme. She occupied rooms at the top of the octagon tower, at the end of the long gallery. It was an ideal vantage point with long views in three directions. She planted the famous yew tree in 1659. At least one visitor, having seen Skipton Castle featured in a television series called Treasure Hunt, asked to be shown the yew tree planted by presenter Anneka Rice!

Standing by the chapel, I wondered why Lady Anne, a most devout woman, should have failed to restore this building when everything else had been renewed. It may be because she had spent freely on restoring the nearby parish church where the bones of some of her ancestors, including her father, recline in richly carved and colourful tombs on either side of the altar.

As for the chapel, it became a secular building. Within easy memory are the days when it was a barn and a shippon. Cows were milked in stalls set against the wall in which are the remains of a once splendid east window. Lady Anne would not have approved.

Skipton Castle, home of Lady Anne Clifford

The Romantics and the Dales

In spring 1990, when I was taking an evening history course in Settle, number eighteen in the series was entitled 'The Romantics'. It related to the period between 1760 and 1820 when the caves, crags and chasms of High Craven were visited by people of taste and leisure.

When looking for sublimity, the Romantics found it in popular caves and also in a gloriously visible limestone feature such as Gordale Scar at the head of Malhamdale. Thomas Gray (1769) was greatly impressed by the waterfall. He wrote about what he referred to as The Scar which 'overshadows half the area below with its dreadful canopy where I stand'. John Hutton (1781), a Kendal clergyman, was fascinated by caves in the Ingleton district. He responded with some emotion. His mind was also capable of assessing scientific fact. In his book, *Tour of the Caves*, he rightly deduced from fossil evidence in high places that the limestone had a marine origin. Then, being a cleric, he reconciled this with the Biblical story of the Flood.

Guides at the caves included William Wilson, an old soldier who lit up the calcite formations with lanthorn and candlestick. Houseman (1800) went with Wilson to Yordas Cave where the guide 'now places himself upon a fragment of the rock and strikes up his lights consisting of six or eight candles, put into as many holes of a stick'. Each, fixed at the tip of a long pole, meant that he could 'illuminate a considerable space'.

Using a 'Claude Glass' the Romantics studied a reflection of the landscape – on which they turned their backs. This also applied to unnatural but magnificent features such as Bolton Priory, in Wharfedale. At Bolton Abbey some early English landscape painters – Girtin, Copman and Turner – set down their impressions in a freer, more colourful way than had been the custom in painting. There was a demand for ruins, particularly those decked with ivy and having a tinge of romance.

By 1830, the Romantic Age was waning and in 1837, with the discovery of the further reaches of Clapham Cave, at the head of well-watered Clapdale, the scientific aspect was being stressed. The first-known potholers were John Birkbeck and William Metcalfe.

Arts

JB in the Dales

'I am glad that our beloved Dales are to have their own magazine and I wish the venture the success it deserves.'

With these words, in the springtime of 1939, JB Priestley offered success to *The Yorkshire Dalesman*, as the magazine was first known. Priestley's mind flashed back to the springtime of 1919. After army service, he related, his very first job was to prepare some articles on a 'little walking tour in the Dales' for a Yorkshire newspaper. 'I went, treading on air, a civilian again ... through Upper Wharfedale and then roaming about in Wensleydale.'

My encounter with Priestley, a literary lion, was in exceptional circumstances – the front room of a terraced house in Settle, 'down t' snicket by t' post office'. It was the springtime of 1965. I did not normally return home at lunchtime. This visit proved to be exceptional. A flustered Freda, my wife, wearing a baking apron, met me at the front door. I heard the voices of two small children in the background. Said Freda, with a

tremor of excitement, 'There's JB Priestley and Jacquetta Hawkes in the front room.'

JB had squeezed into an easy chair. He had removed his black beret. No smoke rose from the pipe he held. Jacquetta was partly obscured by a piano. After being introduced, she left, heading for Victoria Cave on the limestone hills which were visible from my window. JB soon broached the subject of a meal. He asked me to recommend an eating place – nowt posh. I left him at the Wenhaven Café and he clambered up steep steps into an eating place not unlike a café in one of his Yorkshire novels.

I took him to Townhead to meet Tot Lord and see his collection of ancient relics from local caves. He smiled wryly when I showed him a single bone of dubious origin. It was labelled Bone of Contention. Tot gave him a tour of the museum before I offered to drive JB to Clapham to meet Harry Scott at *The Dalesman* office. My car was an ancient Ford, similar in its decrepit state to that James Herriot

JB Priestley

described in his vet books. We occupied seats of a non-Ford origin, set in a floor put in by a Lakeland joiner when the old one was giving way. As I drove up Buckhaw Brow, in a fug of pipe smoke, I prayed that I would not be the person responsible for killing JB Priestley!

I left him with Harry Scott, another keen pipe-smoker. I could barely see across the room for pipe smoke. It was arranged that I would visit JB and his wife at Bainbridge on the following day so I might chat and photograph him. He would then be featured in *The Dalesman* once again.

I arrived early in the day. Sunlight flooded one of the most attractive Dales villages. As I stood outside the local inn, I noticed that a bedroom window was open. There was the tapping of a typewriter and a whiff of smoke. JB, leaning out, arranged to meet me at Muker later in the morning. I crossed Buttertubs and parked opposite the school. We had our chat. Head, shoulder and pipe photographs were taken.

As JB and Jacquetta prepared to set off to enjoy an outdoor painting session, I dashed across to the school, suggesting to the teacher that she might let the children gather at the window to view a literary celebrity.

I was delighted that, through the appeal of *The Dalesman*, I had enjoyed a very special visit.

Great-great Grandad knew the Brontës

Dr William Cartman, my great-great grandfather on my mother's side, included the Brontë family among his friends. He often took services at Haworth Church and dined with the Brontës at the Parsonage. He officiated at the funeral services of both Charlotte and her father. The relationship dated from the time when Patrick was curate at Haworth and William at Bingley.

Cartman cherished his continuing Haworth connection. He often preached from the three-decker pulpit of Haworth Old Church after which he would join Patrick, a widower, and daughter Charlotte for a meal at the vicarage. A generous man, in January 1854 Cartman presented Brontë with an 'ice apparatus' (a pair of heel spikes). In thanking Cartman for his gift, the pastor wrote that he valued it 'as much for the sake of the donor as its own intrinsic worth. It will serve as another prop to Old Age'. Charlotte, in a missive to 'Dear Papa', expressed pleasure that 'you continue in pretty good health' and that 'Mr Cartman came to see you on Sunday'.

Cartman was a close friend of the Rev A B Nicholls, a Haworth curate, and was a calming influence when relations between Patrick Brontë and his curate were strained following his declaration of love for Charlotte. The story, in brief, was that Patrick was against it and Nicholls, repulsed, planned to leave Haworth to preach the gospel in Australia. Minds were changed. Nicholls and Charlotte subsequently had a loving, but very brief, marriage. Charlotte, becoming pregnant, suffered violent nausea which was more than her frail body could stand. She died at the age of thirty-eight. Cartman conducted the funeral service. Patrick sat erect and attentive as Cartman preached from the text, 'And all wept and bewailed her but he said "Weep not, she is not dead but sleepeth".' (Luke 8, verse 52).

Six years later, Cartman returned to Haworth for the funeral of Patrick who died on 7th June 1861, aged eighty-four. The church was packed. Several hundred people thronged the churchyard as the coffin, preceded by the Vicar of Bradford and Dr Cartman, was borne through the eastern gate of the parsonage garden on its way to the church. Lowered into the vault within the altar rails, it came to rest beside the coffin of Charlotte. *The Bradford Review* observed, 'Thus they left Patrick sleeping amidst the ashes of genius.'

The photograph of Cartman that accompanies the article shows a stocky man with a drum-tight stomach. He is clad, like many another Victorian parson, in crow black with a white preaching collar. His frock coat comes down to his knees. He carries a well-brushed top hat and looks contented as he stands in the photographer's studio, with drapes and operatic-type scenery providing a rather stuffy setting. He had doubtless been told not to smile – as if a Victorian parson would think of doing such a thing.

Two walkers in the countryside

'That's a waterfall, isn't it?'

'Weir.'

'Over theer.'

Young Mr Herriot

Having been asked to launch a Dales Craft Trail at Thirsk, I wrote to James Herriot asking if I might have a chat with him earlier in the day. He agreed, by telephone, and it was good to hear the Scottishness in his quiet, well-modulated voice. He was born in Sunderland but reared in Glasgow.

'I'm a city lad,' he remarked as we settled down for a chat. Bodie, a Border Terrier, joined us in the room and lay quietly under his chair. The dog was said to be eight-and-a-half years old but looked older.

Alf Wight, aka James Herriot

The view from Sutton Bank – Alf Wight's favourite in
Yorkshire – overlooked the village where he spent his retirement

'The Border Terriers go white very early. They always look older than they really are.'

I had not seen the vet-turned-scribbler since the launch of his book *James Herriot's Yorkshire* just ten years before. Also at the launch in Leeds was his wife Joan (who became Helen in the Dales stories) and their family, Jimmy and Rosemary.

The James Herriot with whom I now came face to face looked contented and relaxed. His face was a 'good colour' as they say in Yorkshire, partly because he had been out and about in the garden or on the hills during most of the long sunny spell. When I mentioned 'colour' he laughed and recalled his young days as a vet visiting the dalehead farms with their memorable residents:

'When they said you'd a bad colour, you got worried. I'm not a very ruddy individual really but they would say, "Thou's lost a bit o' ground since I last saw you, Mr Wight." Or "I think you've failed a bit, you know".'

James Herriot's introduction to the 'magic land' of the Dales came about when he travelled three times a week to Leyburn to assist the local vet, Frank Bingham, with the tuberculin-testing of cattle.

'Once I got embedded as his helper, he would say, "Oh, while you're there just castrate a couple of colts." Bit by bit I found that I was not only a tester but a practitioner. I got to know every nook and cranny. Right up to Gayle in Wensleydale and to beyond Keld in Swaledale and away up to the head of Coverdale.'

I mentioned that I never motor through Carperby, in Wensleydale, without looking at the Wheatsheaf and recalling the story of the Herriots' unusual honeymoon. It was a 'testing honeymoon'. Alf Wight (the real name of James Herriot) 'hadn't a bean in those days'. The work of tuberculin-testing cows was overdue. So he and his new wife Joan spent part of the time with the livestock, she writing the records and he injecting the cows and calling out their skin measurements. They had been married at Thirsk. They arrived in Carperby after dark and yet Mrs Kilburn and her daughter Gladys were waiting with a hot meal – the first of many memorable meals.

'The farmers were aghast that I should spend part of my honeymoon doing vet's work. Yet it was a very good honeymoon and it was cheap!'

James Herriot drove to the topmost farms in the Dales and met a kind-hearted people.

'The Dales I first knew were teeming with rich characters. The higher you went, the more unique was the type of person you met. I was lucky. Farms were so isolated the people loved to see somebody from the outside world. They were generally large families. After I had done the test they would say, "Come in and 'ave a bit o' dinner." This was the great saying. They were so hospitable. Everyone would 'down tools' and sit round and look at me.'

I asked about Herriot Country. 'I've described it in my book on Yorkshire as the area between two lines drawn from the heads of Coverdale and Swaledale, across the Plain of York and over the Hambleton Hills and the North York Moors to the lovely villages of the coast.'

He decided after his last book, which was published some years ago, that he would give up writing.

'I'm naturally a pretty retiring bloke and I found I was being crushed down by publicity. I thought that the only way to get rid of this was to stop writing. Being a vet was ninety-nine per cent of my time. I'm not an author at all. I'm a vet who scribbled for half an hour after his work at night.'

Meanwhile, the routineless days go quietly by. Sometimes he is working in the garden. Sometimes he goes to his Dales cottage with members of the family and dogs. Sometimes he sets off for the hill with his oldest pal.

'It's very gradual walking. He and I are of the same age. We just walk and chat and put the world to rights.'

Christopher Timothy on location

Christopher Timothy played the part of James Herriot in the BBC series All Creatures Great and Small. I had a friendly chat with him when the team was temporarily established at Askrigg. Our chat took place in a bus with tables, one of a fleet of specialist vehicles parked near the church. He confessed to being 'a bit nervous' during the previous year. He was now more relaxed, having imbibed the atmosphere of the Yorkshire Dales – 'and it's nice'. Having a day off, he and some friends had gone for a picnic in Swaledale. It had been idyllic. 'I live in London. The air and water up here in the Dales are clean which is wonderful for a start. Everywhere I look there is something to catch the eye.' Christopher lived down south but in 1988 had spent a total of eighteen weeks in the Yorkshire Dales. He recalled a tale when Robert Hardy (who plays Siegfried), Peter Davison (Tristan) and he were supposed to leave the 'vet's house' in Askrigg, say cheerio to each other and go their separate ways. About three hundred people were watching the filming. The production assistant was being gentle with them. He opened the door to absolute silence. All the traffic had been stopped. Then across the front of the house walked a woman carrying two shopping baskets. The production assistant asked if she wouldn't mind holding back while the scene was being shot. She gave a loud reply, 'I've got my own bloody life to live!' As Christopher said, 'There was no answer to that. It was her village, not ours!'

I was very much impressed by the way in which the stars of a memorable series dealt with enquiries from the public. I had a brief chat with some of them over a drystone wall. I was on a road, they were in a field, about to be under the eye of the camera. Christopher Timothy made one old woman's day when he gave her a hug before the camera which was being held by her husband. So was recorded a moment to remember – and one for the old lady to relate to wide-eyed neighbours at home.

Christopher Timothy

Cutcliffe Hyne: a huge man, mentally and physically

Twelve years have passed since the death of Charles John Cutcliffe Hyne, novelist creator of *Captain Kettle*, but when I recently visited his old home at Kettlewell I had the feeling that it was only yesterday, for here are the many books he wrote, documents he compiled and treasures collected in all parts of the world.

Cutcliffe Hyne is never far from my thoughts when I wander in the Kettlewell district. If I find myself by one of the small streams which frolic down the slopes to the valley I picture him panning for gold. He actually found it – but not in any quantity that would cause a gold rush. Alternatively, one can ponder his idea for a Dales watercress industry, his keen defence of a local cairn threatened with destruction, his suggestion that the railway should provide camping coaches and his vast scheme for reclaiming Morecambe Bay, which has been silting up for years. His mind teemed with notions and ideas that were not as odd as they seemed at first acquaintance.

Money was not plentiful in his youth and even less so when he was struggling to make his way as a writer. Turning out 12,000 words for one magazine earned him one guinea. Three novels came from his pen but they were not financial successes. For four years he devoted his energy to writing boys' books.

Somehow he must broaden his experience. He yearned to escape from the limitations of his past way of life. Since his boyhood days, he had loved the sea and decided to use this medium for travelling round the world. It became the passion that drove him abroad for around ten thousand miles each year. He was a winch hand on one voyage, the doctor on another. He went to the Arctic, Lapland, the jungles of Brazil and the Congo, and to the Spanish Main. He mined in Mexico and hunted for treasure at Savage Island. He is said to have eaten everything from frilled mule to reindeer and drunk most things from jungle water to queer native brews.

Many characters tripped off the pages of his books but none was more popular than Captain Kettle. *Honour of Thieves* was serialised in a magazine and Kettle was introduced as a small, rather insignificant character. When the last of the articles appeared, Cutcliffe Hyne was told that 'the little red-headed sailor man was the best touch in your story.' After turning down 'thirty bob a thousand words' for a series, he settled on a separate deal and a long saga began. The tales of this colourful personality were spread over about forty years; though, of course, they did not represent his total output by any means.

'I write my stories anywhere,' Cutcliffe Hyne once said. 'I have written them in the Atlas Mountains and leaning against a lamp-post in Bradford.'

Cutcliffe Hyne was a huge man both mentally and physically, standing six feet four inches in his stockinged feet. He was strong and fond of exercise. Among his many loves was shooting, and he had followed the tracks of big game in the African jungles and on tropical plains as well as the less exciting wild animals of his own land.

His daughter gave me some insight into his writing:

'He had quite settled hours. He regarded it as a job and had his meals at the proper time. His was a quiet, orderly, methodical writing life.'

All his writing was accomplished in longhand, with an H pencil, and he left big margins in which he could scrawl additional words. His writing was tiny. Cutcliffe Hyne had a great fondness for animals, especially cats, which would often climb on his shoulders as he wrote.

He was fascinated by Kettlewell and in an article he contributed to the first edition of *The Dalesman* he declared that a historian was wanted for Kettlewelldale:

'It has always been a source of wonder to me why some man or woman with an itch for writing does not dig into the ancient history of Kettlewelldale and clamp it down on paper.'

And in brisk, racy style he created pictures from the long past of 'shambling bipeds' which 'dodged cave tigers and other beasts among the limestone rocks'. Later he spoke about Saxon times when 'the village flitted down from its perch on the Langcliffes to its present site on the floor of the valley.'

He died in March 1944, at the age of seventy-eight, and was buried in the churchyard in Kettlewell.

Television

The TV set at a Wharfedale farm was decrepit. Asked if he was thinking of buying another, the farmer remarked, 'I've nobbut getten used to t'fowk on this set.'

Chapters in a Dales life

Just sixty years ago, Ella Pontefract and Marie Hartley, of Wetherby, formed a writer and artist partnership, rented a disued farmhouse at Angram and gathered material for a book about Swaledale life and traditions. Ella

Joan Ingilby

wrote in her diary that they were staying at a 'funny rambling old house with all the windows facing the wrong way'. Marie recalls:

'When we wanted a bath, we were loaned a tin one, on the understanding that it was returned every Saturday so that Tom, our landlady's youngest child, might have his weekly bath.'

Swaledale, published in 1934, was written by Ella and illustrated by Marie. In 1938, having compiled books on Wensleydale and Wharfedale, they bought Coleshouse, a cottage at Askrigg. Ella died in 1946 at the age of forty-eight. Two years later, Joan Ingilby, herself a poet and writer, joined Marie at her Dales home.

Coleshouse, by the hill road leading from Askrigg into Swaledale, is an unpretentious cottage, built of local materials and fittingly adapted to be the home of writer and artist. Nothing seemed to have changed since my last visit. The wrought-iron gate shut with a clunk, not a clatter.

The garden was spangled with celandines. A burst of sunshine burnished the well-polished door-knocker.

Marie opened the door and the tradition of Dales hospitality was continued by Joan, who offered me a cup of coffee. We sat beside a coal fire, reminiscing about the Dales. It was at the fireside that JB Priestley had relaxed during a four days' stay with Marie and Joan. Television had reached the dale but they rarely switched it on. Courtesy demanded that when Priestley revealed a fondness for televised boxing, he was allowed to watch a match. As the fight progressed, he gave a running commentary.

Now, Marie gave a brief commentary on the events sixty years before when she and Ella had rented the farmhouse to research their Swaledale book. There was not a drop of rain for the whole month. Returning to the valley for a shorter period in October, they completed the work on what is now a classic study of a Yorkshire dale.

They followed the success of Swaledale with a similar study of Wensleydale and, having little spare cash, they operated from a second-hand caravan they had purchased at Otley.

The van, named Green Plover, after the lapwing, a familiar dales bird, was first driven to Shaw Paddock near the source of the Ure and not far from the Settle-Carlisle Railway. Each evening, as the two women went to their beds, a regular steam-hauled express thundered by.

Marie Hartley

Wharfedale completed a trilogy of outstanding books. Ella's death ended the collaboration but the memory lingers on through her diary and published work. In the very first issue of *The Yorkshire Dalesman* she wrote about dalesfolk and quoted a hill farmer, a man with the simple but strong faith of his ancestors, 'If there's another Noah's flood, there won't be many folk left I' England when t'watter comes bashin' down oor chimney pots.'

Marie's collaboration with Joan Ingilby, who lived at North Deighton, three miles from Wetherby, has led to the compilation of many more dales books. Marie has albums of photographs of Dales life dating back to the 1930s. Theirs is a true collaboration. They write a chapter each then exchange them for criticism and revision. Marie told me:

'I am best at the broad sweep of a book. Joan is a stickler for detail. We accept each other's criticism in the right spirit and work in perfect harmony.'

To own a Dales cottage and live by writing is an attractive idea. Most of those who have tried to realise this dream failed, wrongly believing that such a life can be an extensive holiday in pleasant surroundings. Marie and Joan disciplined themselves when recording and writing about the life of their native Yorkshire.

An interview with Marie Hartley appears in the WR Mitchell Archive. Here is an extract.

WRM: What do you feel about the Dales today, looking round? If you were to come into the Dales today writing about them afresh…?

MH: Well, I wouldn't be a writer. I think there's far too much. Everybody's cashing in now, aren't they?

WRM: That's right.

MH: It was very lovely to have the place. It was an open book to us and no one else was writing about it. Nobody had done anything then, you know? Not even *The Dalesman*. That was marvellous. But now everything is trodden ground and Hawes has about fourteen cafés. We used to think Hawes was about the furthest place you could get and now people seem to come in an hour or two and it's crowded out. It hasn't got the old atmosphere as a result, has it? It was just nothing but farmers. We are geared for visitors now, which we weren't. Mind you, it probably saves the day because things aren't too good, are they otherwise? It's now a source of income that one has to consider.

Edward Elgar

Elgar's friendship with a Yorkshire doctor

Writing from Worcester, just before Christmas 1887, the young composer Edward Elgar began a letter with the words, 'My Dear Charles…' The recipient, Charles William Buck, of Settle, was a medical practitioner with a deep love for music, especially that composed for his favourite instrument, the cello. As he wrote, Elgar noted that he was sitting over the fire, his old dog lying at his feet, and that he was 'trying in vain to be cheerful'. He was already familiar with the market town of Settle and with natural features in the limestone countryside around it. He noted that each week, at the railway station in Wells, he scrutinised 'a showboard of Settle as a health resort'. He scanned the old spots with much gusto. Elgar reported to Dr Buck that he had written a vast amount of music that year 'but no money in any of it'.

The friendship between Elgar and Buck extended over some fifty years. They first met at Malvern at a music festival. The friendship ended with the death of Buck at Giggleswick in 1932. Elgar did not long survive him. Letters written by the composer to Buck and his daughter, Monica, are still in existence. They are generally brief and gossipy. Elgar periodically scribbled down music and he was not above drawing on his letters. He sketched in the basic features of a cat to remind Dr Buck's daughter of one seen on the scars (presumably Giggleswick Scars) and another letter had drawings of mice.

Dr Buck's large house overlooked the market place in Settle. He had a small room devoted to music and here he could muster one or two local men – amateur musicians, as he was, all being members of the fine orchestra that accompanied the productions of local operas. Buck was the conductor. It was the period when an amateur society invariably chose to present Gilbert and Sullivan. The performances took place at the Victoria Hall, a few yards from one of the viaducts of the Settle-Carlisle Railway. It throbbed with the passage of many steam-hauled trains.

Elgar stayed with his friend in Settle and, later, at the retirement home in Giggleswick. Each visit was usually short, extending over a few days, undertaken when Elgar was in the north. He might be attending a musical festival in Leeds. The train carried him to Ribblesdale and on some excursions he left the train at Hellifield, being met by someone with a pony and trap.

When Monica Buck was six years of age, Elgar nursed her and the chair on which they sat is still in use at her Cumbrian home. She recalls that her father was fond of collecting local ballads. He recorded the strains to which they were sung and Elgar would later harmonise them. A surviving manuscript book of music bears Elgar's signature. He composed a gavotte which he dedicated to the doctor.

Elgar and Buck played golf on the course set almost in the shadow of Giggleswick Scar. They clambered up the local hills and took pony and trap excursions to local waterfalls. At his Worcestershire home, Elgar was always pleased to hear of musical events being held in Ribblesdale.

When Dr Buck died, the sadness of the ageing Elgar was reflected in the letters he wrote to the doctor's family, letters which, amazingly, have survived to give us an insight into a remarkable and prolonged friendship.

The clouds are mucky: Ashley Jackson

A shley Jackson paints what he sees which means that most of his pictures have mucky clouds and dark, tousled landscape with the cores of old snowdrifts lying against the walls. Ashley is fond of picturing the moorland farms, the crags and solitary trees which wheeze and creak like old men with bronchial trouble. Entering his gallery, I was surrounded by so many moorland scenes I half expected to hear the tinkle of beck water against gritstone or the becking of red grouse.

He was a signwriter (who could not spell too well) before he became an artist. Hankering after art, and painting landscapes with mucky skies, he had his first one-man exhibition at Brighouse and, in due course, began to put down roots at Holmfirth.

Not all his skies have dark tones. One snowscape, with a big sky, features expanses of blue with streaks of vapoury white. No two skies are similar. There is soft light on his study of Widdup Moor, all-over greyness (plus a jumble of telegraph posts and wires) on his study of Underbank Old Road, Holmfirth, and a graduation of even tones on 'Cold and Damp', portraying one of those misty, dismal days, this one experienced at the edge of Bradshaw Moor.

I questioned him about his forbidding skies.

'When painting in the open air,' he replied, 'you have no time to play about. Your skies have to go down quickly and, as in life, it's your first statement that counts. If you have to re-track, then tear the painting up.'

Such an impulse needs a large brush to support it. 'The size of the brushes used are the large Daler Rowney wash brushes.'

When he was commissioned to appear in an art series for the BBC, he told the viewers to protect their brushes, when they were being transported, by dipping them into a jam jar of water containing the white of an egg.

'This will size your brushes, making them hard until they are used again.'

One viewer wrote complaining that the technique did not work.

'It was not until after much investigation that we found he was frying his egg and cutting the white into strips before dropping them into the water.'

Ashley's memories of the Dales are often associated with drizzle, if not rain. Neither deters him from painting when the mood is upon him. A shepherd who approached him on a drizzly day looked at his half-completed landscape for a few minutes and remarked, 'Thou's getten some real clouds. I've sin paintings of this part o' t' Dales where t'clouds turned out like a cow's udder.' Needless to say, none of Ashley Jackson's subsequent work has resembled an udder. An artist does not forget such an observation.

He has a sense of fun and in one of his books mentioned that a 'squirrel hair brush' did indeed come from a squirrel, more precisely the tail. And a sable brush was formed of hair from the tail of a sable. He mentioned that a brush made from hairs plucked from the tail of a Manx cat was rare and was astonished at the number of people who tried to acquire one.

You need a big brush to paint a big, wet Yorkshire sky.

Courting

A courting couple walked across the fields. He said, 'What's ta bin thinkin', lass?'

'Nowt much,' she whispered.

'What? Doan't you think about me?'

'I was.'

Fred Lawson

Fred was born in Yeadon in 1888. He visited Castle Bolton, in Wensleydale, on a month's holiday in 1910 and never wanted to leave, having realised an ambition to live by clean streams.

'I loved those craggy bits at the edge of moors where there is water rushing down to the valley.'

Fred adopted Wensleydale and commended its beauty in quick sketches and magnificent paintings, mainly in watercolour. He preferred to look down on a valley rather than up to the hills. And he walked to chosen vantage points, observing, 'I've found out that people who have cars to carry their stuff do very little painting. They are always looking for something better further along the road. When you're walking, there's a limit to how far you can go.'

Fred had made long jaunts to the Continent but in later life he rarely wandered more than ten miles from home. He was an all-weather painter and the most unpretentious artist I have met. He donned an old jacket and, on chilly days, he swaddled himself with sacks. A battered hat protected his head from the vagaries of the Dales weather.

His home at Castle Bolton was also his studio and art gallery. The studio was used infrequently. He would point to the landscape beyond and say, 'That's my studio.'

He was to marry Muriel Metcalfe, an artist in her own right. 'His hands were small and I was fascinated to see him using them when drawing or painting. He was inspired and did not rely on a set method. Fred was very much himself. The lines flowed. He loved wildness and the snow.'

On the day Fred proposed to her he was painting the fair at Leyburn. 'He loved the colour, movement and excitement of fairgrounds, which were set up in the Dales on old feast days. I sauntered up the town and there he was, just finishing his picture, putting it down carefully so no one would tip it over. He had brought his old briar pipe out of his pocket to have a smoke. He leaned against a town hall windowsill. I was just eighteen years old but we talked as equals for a minute or two. In the background, the roundabout was operating, the music blaring. Fred just looked at me and said, "Will you marry me?" Just like that. He was absolutely straight and, of course, I said yes.'

Fred had a regular series in *The*

Dalesman. Each month, he sent a scribbled letter and sent a hastily drawn picture. Our readers loved to see them. When I queried what I had taken to be Fred's first abstract drawing, accompanying one of his letters, he replied, 'Nay, it's a bit o' plaster on the wall in our outside privy.'

Fred died in 1968. JB Priestley wrote, 'He lived in the Dales, he knew and loved the Dales and he drew and painted what he saw, year after year, all around him.'

Thelma Barlow

Thelma's entry to Coronation Street was modest. She was cast as a friend of Emily Nugent, who was to become engaged to Ernest Bishop. 'Poor Mavis was a friend of hers who was rather peeved because Emily was getting engaged before her. So she had a couple of sherries in quick succession and got a little tiddly, had a tearful scene – and left!' That was until, a year later, Emily was to marry Ernest. Thelma was invited to appear in two further episodes. She was asked back for six weeks and then written into the script as Mavis Riley, the self-conscious and indecisive spinster. 'That was 14 years ago.'

The personalities of Thelma and Mavis are not alike at all. Thelma, as befits her Yorkshire upbringing, has a clear vision of life and of her own progress through it. She has a sense of adventure that Mavis would have admired. In 1986, she and a friend spent several days walking in the footsteps of the Himalayas.

In her Dales setting she is quietly accepted by local people who do not make a fuss and allow her to lead a relaxing life away from the stresses of her work. She is well-disposed towards the community, helps where she can and even took part in a sponsored boundary walk, the money from which went towards the re-roofing of the church. Her house, a converted barn, is just off the tourist routes. The view takes in fields, a pattern of drystone walls and a moorland ridge, beyond which is Bowland.

Hard Work

Hard wark's killed neabody, but thowt's on it's killed mony a thoosand.

Wildlife and Nature

Richard Kearton

Richard Kearton was proud of his Dales background. He came from yeoman stock, his family had owned land in Swaledale since the fourteenth century. While staying with some old Yorkshire friends near Enfield, Kearton found a song thrush nest. He invited his brother, Cherry, to photograph it with a cheap second-hand camera he had just bought. The result was so full of promise, Richard produced a book on birds' nests, illustrating it entirely with photographs taken 'direct from nature'. Those three words were to be the theme of the brothers' later work. In short, and by chance, Richard Kearton became the father of natural history photography.

The editor of an illustrated weekly paper accepted an article and pictures. With the projected book on nests in mind, the brothers set out on a remarkable series of journeys. What was refreshingly new about the Kearton brothers was the way they featured the efforts they made to obtain pictures. Cherry, the athletic one, was portrayed descending a cliff,

among other situations. There was humour in a picture of the famous stuffed ox being borne into the countryside and of Cherry standing on Richard's shoulders, attending to a camera they had placed on an enormous tripod.

To obtain pictures for *British Birds' Nests* they climbed trees, scaled cliffs, ascended mountains and sailed to remote Scottish islands. In fifteen years, Richard and Cherry travelled over 30,000 miles and exposed over 10,000 photographic plates. The book was published in 1895.

Richard died in 1928, aged sixty-six. He was facing his third serious illness. One had crippled him as a child, the next forced his retirement to the country. Ralph Chislett, a notable Yorkshire ornithologist, assessed the work of Richard Kearton as follows:

'By books, pictures and lectures, he did more than anyone else to direct the new and growing interest in natural history into the right channels. Among bird photographers he remains the classic master of his art.'

Their work was marked by tenacity, patience and enterprise.

'The great secret of all field work is to keep absolutely still for a prolonged period of time,' wrote Richard. 'My brother waited a whole day for a picture of a vole on one occasion. On another, he spent six days in patient waiting and watching for a series of studies on the kingfisher.'

They groaned under the weight of photographic material. They worked with a five-inch by four-inch field camera which had a nine-inch rectilinear lens and a roller-blind shutter. The speed of the plates they used was frustratingly low.

Richard was anxious to obtain pictures of birds without disturbing them. The first attempts were bizarre, involving hides such as a hollow ox and sheep. They even had an 'artificial rock'. Richard subsequently discovered that the actual shape did not matter. Any hollow structure was suitable providing it was not suddenly dumped beside a nest. It must be put down at a distance and moved nearer on successive visits.

A Kearton-type hide

Legacy of Yorkshire's natural history boys

The Ilkley lad who half a century ago sat through lectures of the Wharfedale Naturalists, his lower jaw drooping with astonishment, was Alan Titchmarsh. After a long and varied gardening career, much of it spent under the unblinking stare of the television camera, Alan recently presented Britain's landscape and wildlife on the television screen, in glorious colour.

It was timely. The BBC Natural History Unit had attained its fiftieth anniversary. With Ilkla' Moor as a backdrop to his earlier life, Alan must have felt comfortable during the filming of the moorland part of his natural history series. We were shown 'becking' cock grouse, with which he had been familiar since boyhood. An inert chick was seen to be located but left alone in its mini-jungle of heather by a sporting dog.

On the Cairngorms, Alan lay within a foot or two of a dotterel covering a clutch of eggs like a feathered tea-cosy. In their spring migration, from south of the Mediterranean, to hill ranges much further north, some dotterel touch down for a few days on Pendle Hill, Ingleborough and Cross Fell, the highest point of the Pennines.

Alan's television series, The Nature of Britain, gave a new slant to an old topic. For me, it brought to mind other north-country naturalists.

I thought of Norman Frankland, stalwart of the Craven Naturalists, who located a holly fern for me. It grew in an old scree. As we prepared to leave, Norman partly covered it so that it would not be conspicuous to plant collectors.

Peter Delap, who lived in Cumbria but knew Yorkshire wildlife well, especially the Bowland sika deer, described himself as 'doctor deerologist'. He was the perfect companion when deer-watching, arresting the attention of roebuck by imitating a range of gruff sounds.

Into my mind, as I pondered on Yorkshire naturalists of old, came the name of Chris Cheetham, naturalist extraordinary. I knew him rather more than half a century ago. The first time we went botanising, Chris and I

Bill ready for a date with nature

trampled from Austwick towards the wooded slopes of Oxenber. I ranged over a field looking for splashes of floral red, yellow or blue. He knelt on the ground and pointed out a dozen inconspicuous species of plant in an area the size of my handkerchief. Chris was born in 1875 and was, therefore, as old as the Yorkshire Naturalists' Union, of which he was secretary. He took out full membership in 1905 and had kept all the membership cards since that date. He retired from textile designing in 1934 and moved to Austwick. Henceforth, he never shaved and habitually wore shorts.

Arthur Rufus Sanderson, who lived at Austwick Hall, aroused Chris's interest in catching and identifying two-winged flies. Chris had cases of specimens, some so small you could not make anything of them with the naked eye. A species of daddy-longlegs was named after him: *Tipula cheethami*.

When Chris focused his attention on mosses and lichens, years elapsed before he felt to have caught up with the knowledge gained by one of his heroes, John Nowell, who was born in 1802. This Todmorden handloom weaver and botanist was so poor he had to walk on all his rural expeditions.

At the age of twelve, Chris had received from an uncle one of the first safety bicycles. From that day, he used cycles exclusively during his journeys and to attend YNU meetings. He reckoned to have biked half-a-million miles and asserted that cycle travel was the only proper way of moving about the countryside. When he was over seventy years old and his mother was in her nineties, he took her for rides on a tandem. Chris attended both church and chapel on a Sunday. He liked a good sing. The last time I walked with this fine naturalist was to Oxenber. As usual, he continually picked up specimens of plant life and, handing them to me, asked me to taste them. He was careful when choosing a route for the descent of Oxenber. When he had broken a hip in a fall, an artificial replacement was provided. The surgeon might have left a hole through which the metal joint might be oiled.

Yorkshire has many natural history groups which advance our knowledge of the environment, so vital when the perils of global warming are becoming evident. Alan Titchmarsh, the Ilkley lad who had his fascination with plants and wild life awakened by Wharfedale Naturalists, showed by his appearance in his latest television series there are places where nature still has the upper hand.

Evenings with barn owls

You might have heard the story of the dalesman and a friend from the city who were walking at the 'edge of dark' when a weird sound was heard. The city man queried which creature had made such a blood-curdling sound. The dalesman said, 'It was an owl.' 'I know that,' was the reply, 'but what was 'owling?' If any sound is calculated to send six-inch shivers down the spine of a stranger, it is that of the barn owl, a creature which flies through the half-light like a big white moth.

The powerful talons of a barn owl. Photo by Greg Hume

I spent many an evening watching barn owls before the lusty growth of one of our brave new conifer forests could clag the landscape with an impenetrable mass of trees and deprive the good earth of light. Such forest is seen in Widdale, near Hawes, and in a great arc around the northern side of Penyghent. In the forest I visited, with permission of course, several owl pairs were nesting in old farmsteads and barns which stood incongruously with a stubble of young sitka spruce around them. The birds I watched were in a small barn at the edge of the forest. The adult birds divided their food-hunting time between the dark alleys between the trees and rough pastureland visited by scarcely any creature but sheep and nesting birds. The forest was benevolent to owls. It rustled with short-tailed field voles whose runs, canopied by the ungrazed grass, were found everywhere. They left piles of bright green droppings as a minute offering to the fertility of the ground.

I used a hide of wood and hessian which could be approached, latterly on all fours, through an area of well-grown trees. In the early evening, stimulated into activity by the hunger cries of the young, the adults put in an appearance. I expected to see the cock bird first. It perched on a window ledge, shuffling its feathers while it blinked the last of the sleep mist from its lustrous eyes.

There were evenings of brilliant sunshine and others when rain fell as if from a celestial hosepipe. I settled in the hide with binoculars, coffee in a flask and midge cream in a handy dispenser. On the warm, still evenings, the midges danced and if I were to kill one, a hundred friends turned up for the funeral. The hunger-cries of the owlets formed a light, rhythmic 'snoring' which seemed to be synchronised to the slow beating of my heart. I tried to shake off the desire to slumber by watching a kestrel as it hovered over the dark green pyramids of spruce. The vacuum in owl activity was filled by a chevron of oystercatchers high overhead and by the beginning of what would be a considerable movement of gulls to a roost on water just over the hill. The last of the sunlight edged the gulls' white feathers with a rosy hue.

The owlets renewed their calling and the hint was taken by the cock bird. Suddenly it was in view – an apparition in white, its wings buff and mottled with grey, staring at the forest with eyes like black grapes set in a heart-shaped facial disc above the hooked beak which marked the bird out as a predator. This bird's feathers looked ragged after weeks of attending to the young. The head revolved as if on castors. The eyes of a barn owl are fixed in their sockets. Because of their large size, they provide good binocular vision for rapid descent on to the prey. But they make it necessary for the neck to be turned if the owl is to look round. I had forgotten about the hen bird until she appeared at the ledge and joined in the search for food. A shuttle service operated for the next hour or so.

On the last day of my vigil, as summer died, a young owl showed itself on the window ledge. Others appeared. They almost ravaged the returning birds. I will long remember the first flight because two of them alighted on my hide. I was sitting with my head less than a foot from where their talons had pierced the hessian.

Owls no longer nest in the old barn at the edge of the forest. The building was demolished. The forest is now so tall and dense that I would find difficulty in moving through. Nesting sites for owls have declined and so has the population, by seventy per cent in the last sixty years.

The farming family who built up a stock of deer

Sika deer, introduced to Gisburne Park by Lord Ribblesdale, were hunted in the hope of being recaptured and returned on the end of the day. A goodly number ran free. Arthur Hodgson, who farmed New Ing near Bolton-by-Bowland, built up a stock over many years. One haytime he came across a recumbent sika calf in a hayfield. It was nurtured by his daughter, Adele.

I enjoyed watching deer in Bowland and the Ribble Valley. The prime times for observation were dawn and dusk when the deer and I might have large tracts of land to ourselves. In autumn, rutting time, the air shivered with the whistling of the deer, each whistle rising and falling, a lovely crescent of sound. Amorous stags, using their antlers as spades, created depressions in wooded areas. The depressions became saucer-like and muddy. A stag rolling in mud

Adele Hodgson with Bambi

was keen to transmit its particular scent by rubbing its antlers against vegetation and trees.

The Hodgsons came into the sika story in a curious way. Arthur and Doreen had moved into the area in 1951. At haytime in 1968 there was a frustrating moment for Arthur. He was riding a tractor, mowing grass in a meadow. The cutter broke down. Arthur raised himself above his seat to see what lay before the tractor. Two feet ahead, in an unmown patch of grass, was the recumbent form of a sika deer calf. Its mother would presumably have been in a nearby tract of woodland. The calf was moved from the tractor's path and mowing continued.

On the following evening, daughter Adele, out walking with Twister, their Dalmatian dog, was surprised when it began to bark. The deer calf was still in the area. It had clearly lacked motherly attention, had a flattened stomach and suffered from exhaustion. The only possibility was for Adele to pick up the calf, named Bambi, and take her back to the farm. She quickly became very tame.

'She followed us round the farm and occasionally met some of her own kind. She never rushed to join them. When stags approached, she ran back to us.'

There was an exception. In April 1971 it was clear that Bambi was in calf.

In due course, Bambi had the shelter of a hut standing in a large enclosure. When Arthur visited at two in the morning during springtime, Bambi was giving birth. Other members of the Hodgson family gathered. They saw a thin, leggy calf stand and take its first steps. Adele remarked, 'Looking at the daughter of Bambi we realised how remarkable it was to have achieved the mating of a wild sika stag and a hind brought up in captivity.'

Bambi, taken into the countryside and mated with wild stags, gave birth in successive years to Kiki, Heidi, Sika and Kochi. In 1975, the irrepressible Bambi produced her first male offspring, which was named Solomon.

I enjoyed my visits to New Ing which, lying at the end of a longish lane, was nicely away from the highly-developed world. I chatted with Arthur, a cheery man, brimming over with life. The Hodgsons did not keep the deer commercially. None was killed for venison or sold to landowners. When Arthur decided to retire from farming, he wondered what should happen to his herd of twenty-two. He wrote to the Queen. She kindly put him in touch with the Royal Zoological Society. A home was found for the deer. Arthur, delighted with the news, died knowing that good care would be taken of them.

Gardening's own rock legend

A flower – the bird's-eye primrose – is the logo of the Yorkshire Dales Society. The inspiration sprang from words written by Reginald Farrer in his book *My Rock Garden* which was published a century ago. To Farrer, bird's-eye primrose was 'my best friend among English wild flowers' being 'such a gallant little thing', fragrant, dainty, lovable with Ingleborough as 'the centre of distribution'.

Reginald John Farrer was brought up at Ingleborough Hall, Clapham. A delicate and lonely lad, he passed many a day in spring clambering about the crags and scars of Ingleborough seeking rare plants. In his mature years, Farrer popularised rock gardening, setting aside many old ideas. For his own enterprises, large quantities of limestone were moved by horse and sled from the heights of Ingleborough, a practice that would be abhorred today. Farrer's prose style, displayed in many books, was enchanting. He noted that two absolute essentials for a rock garden are an open situation and perfect drainage. 'A dank hollow is doom; drip is damnation.'

From old folk in Clapham in the 1950s, I heard about the delightful eccentricities of Reginald Farrer. He lived at a time when strange but attractive plants, collected in many parts of the world, were enriching English gardens. Farrer was exceptional. Unlike other famous plant-hunters he had not gone through a rigorous training in botanic gardens or nurseries.

Weakly as a lad, with a hare-lip and cleft palate, which he later concealed behind a bushy moustache, Reginald grew up at a time when his mother Elizabeth, with a large and inexpensive labour force, was re-styling the hall grounds. Farrer's wanderlust took him to the alpine areas of Europe and the Far East.

He might be working in his garden when, suddenly and still in gardening togs, he would set off for the railway station one and a half miles away. When next heard of he would be in London. He would contact his mother for money and other requirements before departing on a plant-hunting expedition.

James Farrer, his father, was rather dull and self-centred. Elizabeth, his doting mother, small and dumpy, not unlike Queen

Victoria, radiated good spirits. She saw to it that Reginald had a good supply of his favourite food, peppermint creams and tinned sausages, which he would consume when he was on some remote Far Eastern mountains, in mist and rain.

Just a century ago, when *The Rock Garden* was published, Farrer renounced the faith of his fathers and became a Buddhist. His religious impulses were finely-focused during a visit to Ceylon. In Clapham, when Farrer put on a slide show for the villagers, he wore eastern garb and spoke with a high, squeaky voice.

I broached the subject of Farrer with Geoffrey Smith, a celebrated gardener, who was then at Harlow Carr Gardens, Harrogate. He considered that Farrer was a genius. He altered the course of gardening, transforming, in particular, the art of the rock gardener. Alan Bennett, who has a house at Clapham, wrote a foreword for my little book about Farrer. He thought that considering his contribution to botany and in the light of today's gardening fever, it's surprising that Reginald Farrer's somewhat sad life is not better known.

Farrer died while plant-hunting in Upper Burma and was buried near the Burmese hill fort at Konglu. Mr Hazzard, for years the sub-postmaster at Clapham, told me that when he delivered the telegram announcing his death to his mother at Ingleborough Hall, she was naturally distraught. A memorial was erected in a plot lying just off the main terrace. Not long before he died, he had sent home a consignment of seeds. They included two hitherto rare rock plants that now bear his name: *Gentiana farreri* and *Lilium farreri*.

My favourite Farrer story was told to me by Fred Loads, a former broadcaster on gardening topics who visited what had been the Craven Nursery at Clapham in 1950.

Farrer loved Siamese cats, prefixing each by the name 'Princess'. When, from London, he notified George Redman, his gardener, that the body of a princess had been dispatched by rail to Clapham and that he must arrange for a tomb to be built on the hillside, George took this literally. He hired a cab and, thinking to collect the body of a princess with due style and reverence, took along with him the village clergyman, complete with cassock and surplice. As the train arrived, they stood to attention on the platform. The guard handed them a small coffin, about two feet long. This Princess was, indeed, a cat.

There's Methodism in my Madness

Pulpit tales of the Yorkshire Dales

My mobility for preaching appointments was sustained by walking, by bus and a bike that squeaked and rattled. Keeping appointments on a Sunday, when public transport was limited, was not easy, until I purchased a low-powered motor cycle. This had an expansive transparent screen to break the back of a breeze. It also slowed me up!

A preacher friend who cycled to his appointments found, one day, he had to counter a head wind. He quietly prayed that it would change direction. It did. It was against him when he cycled home after the service.

In Malhamdale, I used a Pennine bus at the beginning and end of the venture and, in between, walked for a few miles. The first stage was from Skipton to Airton, a village some ten miles to the north-west. After taking the morning service, I walked up to the hamlet of Calton and dined with an old lady, a spinster distantly related to Dad. I found myself in a delightfully old-fashioned house, and ate under the gaze of a young man and woman whose images had been fixed in oil by a celebrated Kendal artist. The young man in the painting was, reputedly, a minor officer in the fleet of Admiral Lord Nelson at Trafalgar. Before I could check this, the owner had died and the paintings vanished from my sight. In the days before electrical refrigerators became common, I was taken into the cellar and shown the hole where conditions were sufficiently chilling for ice cream to be produced, thanks to a deep-seated spring.

From Calton, I walked along the eastern side of the River Aire up to Malham, admiring the appearance and manner of a dipper, a bird with deep brown plumage and a white frontal patch. I reached Malham in time to take the afternoon and evening services. There might even be time to walk to the Cove.

Local preachers who did not have their own transport listened during the latter part of the evening service for sounds that indicated that the last bus of the day was entering the village. It would be arranged that he or she might leave the pulpit to catch it for the return to Skipton. A member of the congregation would then pronounce the Benediction.

The last service I took was at Newby Chapel. It was a special occasion. Almost every inch of pew space was occupied. I spoke about preaching in pulpits in various parts of Britain, one of them being the Methodist chapel at Haroldswick, Shetland, the most northerly place of worship in the land. Freda and I had walked from the chapel across a skua-infested terrain to a cliff-edge from which I could view Muckle Flugga, the most northerly point in Britain.

Old-style Methodism

My grandfather was a Methodist local preacher of t'owd-fashioned sort. His faith was rock hard. He loved to smoke a pipe but one day, while walking beside the Aire, he had a feeling that God did not want him to smoke. He took the pipe from his mouth and tossed it into the river.

My father, also a local preacher, once took a service at Barden, in Wharfedale. The chapel-keeper, whose living quarters were at ground-floor level, was also the society steward and organist. As she passed the pulpit on the way to the organ, she whispered: 'Cut thee sermon short when tha' smells t'Yorkshire pudding.'

Many tales are told of local preachers. Typical is of the member of the flock who said, 'I had a locust preacher to tea t'other Sunday.' Her friend corrected her. 'It's local, not locust preacher. A locust settles in a place and eats all afore it.' The first speaker replied, 'Aye, that's what this chap did.'

When I showed nervousness in a Dales vestry before the service, a steward remarked: 'Nay, lad – we should be freightened o' thee. Not thee of us!'

For many years, a small army of cheerful volunteers addressed congregations with easy informality. When the Prodigal Son returned home, having 'spent up', he had been driven to feeding swine. A Nidderdale preacher said, 'And soa t' lad came 'ome agean – and he was all clarted up wi' pig muck.'

For seven years in the 1950s, home was the village of Austwick. The chapel organ was hand-pumped with old Mr Batty as the organ-blower. His guide as to how much air remained in the bellows was a piece of lead, dangling on a string, with the words 'empty' and 'full' marked on the adjacent woodwork. Above the word 'full' some wit had scribbled 'bust'.

Methodists like a good sing, especially to a familiar tune. Malcolm Skidmore, well known throughout the Dales as an auctioneer, told me the story of the preacher who, hearing the unfamiliar strains from the harmonium, said to the lady organist, 'Can we have a more up-to-date tune?' She replied, 'You can't have anything more up-to-date than this. I'm makkin it up as I goes on.'

We had our moments of high emotion at Austwick when a local quarryman uttered rousing 'Hallelujahs' and 'Amens' if a preacher made a particularly telling point. The quarryman sometimes disagreed with what was being said and in this case shouted, 'No, lord'.

Keasden was the only chapel where I was heckled. I remember that springtime day well. Curlews hung briefly in the air like feathered kites before going into their song glides. One settled on the capstone of a wall a proverbial stone's throw away from the chapel. Inside the building, every pew was occupied. On a front pew were several carrycots holding well-mannered babies. For some reason, the oldest men occupied the back pew. I began

my Children's Address, which admittedly was a little fanciful. An old chap rose shakily to his feet and said in stentorian tones he would use when calling in the cows, 'We want none o' thee fairy tales 'ere.' It was these same men who, if they disagreed with something a preacher had said during his sermon, afterwards discussed it with him in the vestry.

After almost two hundred years of powerful witness in the Dales, Methodism is waning. At some chapels a lively fellowship remains. At many others, on Sunday, the footfalls of the Faithful Few rouse the echoes. Many chapels have closed. Barden Chapel, where my father brought his sermon to a close when he smelt t' Yorkshire pudding, is now a craft centre.

The new curate mentioned by mistake that Christ had fed the five thousand with two thousand loaves and two small fishes. A Dales farmer remarked, 'That's nowt. I could have done it.' Next Sunday, the curate correctly quoted 'two loaves and five small fishes'. He leaned over the pulpit and said to the farmer, 'I don't think you'd find that so easy now.' He replied, 'I'd use t'bread left ower frae last Sunday.'

Mr Parker's favourite hymn

Described in Bill's diary as a 'great favourite of mine' and 'my favourite hymn'.

To several generations of West Riding folk, Deep Harmony was a very special hymn tune, used widely by choirs and brass bands. The famous Black Dyke Mills popularised it by playing it after every concert. At its most celebrated period, Deep Harmony was recorded on gramophone records and played often, by special request, on 't' wireless'. For me it evokes images of the old West Riding with its mills, chapels and countless amateur music-makers.

Handel Parker was born at Oxenhope, in a family with strong Haworth connections.

Nearly all the Parkers were musical. Handel's father, Abraham, knew the Brontë family well and was an exponent of the clarinet and violin as well as singing tenor. Charlotte Brontë, when a young girl, is said to have occasionally called at the Parker home and played on Abraham's harmonium. Handel's mother, Martha, had been christened at Haworth in 1825 by the Rev. Patrick Brontë. Her fine voice did not desert her until her dying day, at the age of eighty-five. She sang for the doctor attending her in her last illness

and is reported to have 'hit the top notes'.

Abraham and Martha named their children after individuals who had become famous in the musical world. After the first-born, Handel, followed Miriam, Jubal, Haydn, Frederick and Sarah. Frederick was to have been christened Mozart but, according to Lavinia, Handel's daughter, the name was changed when a neighbour said it 'sounded like Noah's Ark'.

As a small boy, Handel practised on the harmonium by candlelight long after his parents had gone to bed. They must have been tolerant folk as someone once described the harmonium as 'an ill-wind that nobody blows any good'.

At the age of seven, Handel was playing flute in the Oxenhope Drum and Fife Band. By ten, he had obtained his first appointment as an organist.

Handel started work in t'mill but, aged twenty, left for a full-time musical career spanning sixty years. Deep Harmony was composed in 1867, nearly forty years before it was first published when the piece appeared in a collection of Parker's hymns. The name of the tune is said to have been drawn from a friend who, hearing it, remarked, 'By gum, Handel, that's got a deep harmony.'

Handel made scarcely anything out of his hymn-writing. He died a relatively poor man. The funeral service was in Shipley Parish Church. In accordance with Handel's wish, a combined choir sang two hymns to music he had composed. One was a setting to Abide with Me. The other was, of course, Sweet is the Work to the tune – Deep Harmony.

The only picture of
Handel Parker

Suffering from Settle-Carlitis

The railway in the clouds

Settle-Carlitis is an incurable disease. The sufferers do not wish to be cured. I was first afflicted over forty years ago when I wandered into the waiting room at Ribblehead, saw a harmonium – 'an ill wind which nobody blows any good' – inquired about why it was there and became fascinated by tales told of those who made and sustained this railway in the clouds.

My godfather, one of the drivers who thrashed the old steam locomotives up the Long Drag from Settle, fed me with good stories such as that of the old lady living near the line who ensured she had a supply of free coal by placing a row of bottles on her garden wall, confident that no fireman could

Bill in the cab of a steam train

resist lobbing some coal at them.

I coined the term Settle-Carlitis in 1962. The symptoms are a fevered brow, palpitations and an urge to watch the local trains, preferably steam-hauled but, if needs must, even the unspectacular Pacer. There might be a spell of a few weeks when Settle-Carlitis lies dormant. Then, with a whiff of train smoke, the toot of a whistle or yet another spiffing yarn about the line, S-C returns.

Cover of Bill's book on the Settle-Carlisle Railway, The Long Drag

The runaway

An iron-ore train ran backwards from Blea Moor all the way down the line to Long Preston. It was during the Second World War and the loop was full at Blea Moor. The signalman was backing the train across the tracks when a sudden jerk broke the coupling behind the engine. As the trucks started running away, the guard leapt off, helplessly watching as the guards van and eighteen or twenty wagons went off as steady as an express.

At Stainforth, the signalman left the box, expecting a collision. Emergency signals were set at other boxes. The biggest shock was to a group of platelayers who had the sudden appearance of wagons led by a guards van but no engine. The runaways came to a halt some sixteen miles away, at Long Preston.

The spectacular Ribblehead Viaduct

A quest for the shanties

Towards the end of a tinder-dry summer, in 1976, the vegetation had died where the soil was thin. A yellowish pattern appeared on the grass near the road junction at Ribblehead, delineating the foundations of a century-old railway hutment.

The Settle-Carlisle Railway was driven through the hill country between Ribblesdale and the Eden Valley in the 1870s, and so meagre was the accommodation at farm and cottage that the contractor could hold his large labour force only by providing long wooden huts. Groups of huts appeared on the moor between Batty Green and the summit of Blea Moor. They became known as 'shanty towns'.

By the summer of 1870, when over 100 huts had already been erected between Batty Green and Dent Head, a visitor noted that 'human dwellings have sprung up like mushrooms'. The number of huts slowly rose. Eventually, over 2000 people – men, women and many children – lived in an area which had previously been the home of a few farmers, shepherds and gamekeepers.

Outlandish names were given to the shanties. Jerusalem and Jericho were among them and they were topographically correct, Jerusalem having the highest elevation. Anyone who took the local road to Jericho splashed through Pennine bogs and had his legs whipped by heather and rush.

Sebastopol and Inkerman were names familiar to those who had followed our fortunes in the Crimean War. Belgravia was the home of families who regarded themselves as somewhat superior to the common herd. Salt Lake, to the south, was a name far-famed through the zest of the Mormons who had established Salt Lake City and then sent missionaries to the Dales in their efforts to populate it.

The largest shanty town, Batty Green, was in the position handiest to the existing roads. Known in the early days as Batty Wife Hole or Batty Moss, it sprawled at Ribblehead itself, adjacent to the old turnpike from Lancaster to Richmond.

Precisely where did the other places stand? The cleansing Pennine gales long since brushed away the signs of habitation. The year of the Big Drought, 1976, was also the centenary year of the railway. A small group of enthusiasts, the centenary committee, decided as a special study to find out more about the shanties, or 'hut villages' as they were also known.

Into our hands came a report written in the summer of 1872 by a Methodist local preacher. He met Mr Harry Hancock, the railway missionary at Batty Green, and they visited the hutments for hymn-singing, prayer and preaching. Not only were the names of the shanties mentioned, with the exception of Inkerman, a large village whose location remains a mystery, but his description of the tour was detailed enough for us to follow in his footsteps, to use a phrase of which the Victorians were fond.

Mr W H Ashwell, the contractor's agent at Batty Green, provided a horse and trap to take the two men to their first meeting, at Dent Head where a considerable viaduct was being constructed. Those who listened to the men

were casual in the extreme. Many were in shirt sleeves, some were smoking, one held a cat and another held a dog. The shanties swarmed with pets, partly because they also swarmed with rats that, according to one contemporary account, 'have jovial doings among the hut inhabitants' being 'much given to nightly romping above the ceilings'.

So to Batty Green, where acres of ground were covered by temporary buildings. The contractor had established a blacksmith's shop, saw mill, carpenter's shed, stables, pay office and stores. A brickworks, using local materials, produced up to 20,000 bricks a day for the arches of the viaduct and for lining

*Bill with Ribblehead
Viaduct in the background*

Ribblehead Station

the tunnel being made under Blea Moor.

The Methodist preacher did not go into detail about the huts but we discovered from other sources that they were of considerable length, made of wood, roofed with felt that was tarred three times a year. A hut held eight men or, if a family was in residence, there were three rooms: one for the family, one for the lodgers and one used for cooking. One shudders at the thought of the conditions where men alone occupied a hut. They were doubtless squalid. Elsewhere, the women displayed a pride in possession, decorating the rooms with paper hangings and pictures cut from illustrated newspapers and periodicals.

Batty Green had a base for the missionary activity – a room provided by the contractor and opened in December 1870. A bakery produced a maximum of two thousand loaves a day and there was also a slaughterhouse where, each week, they could handle four fat cows, from ten to fifteen sheep and some pigs. Many navvies took nourishment in liquid form, and Batty Green had a brewery and two public houses, but illicit drink was also available from some of the huts. It was written that 'when alcohol and passion rage it becomes dangerous for anyone to interfere'. Interference with the drink

traffic was organised by the Settle Temperance Society, members of which periodically visited the shanty.

The missionaries who visited in 1872 addressed the Sunday School scholars at Batty Green, people who were 'remarkably clean and smartly dressed'. They then followed the two-and-a-half-mile-long tramway, and strode beyond, to visit the few huts on the summit of Blea Moor. Part of a hymn was sung and Mr Hancock 'delivered a few friendly words'. The men returned down the hill and grunted when they met a tradesman with a well-filled pack on his back. Sunday trading, which the missionaries abhorred, was commonplace.

The first drunken navvies were seen at Tunnel Huts. The inebriated men kept their feelings to themselves. More drunken men were seen at Jericho 'but they treated us with much respect'. The inhabitants listened attentively to what the visitors had to say. Then tea was provided. The visitors descended to Sebastopol and its posh suburb. After singing on their progress through Belgravia, they organised an open-air meeting in one of the streets of Batty Green and were then invited to supper.

'Thus we had ample proof that the railway inhabitants on Blea Moor knew how to be courteous and hospitable to strangers.'

When the Scots Express left the rails

The most dramatic moment in Nancy Edmondson's life at Blea Moor was when, age fourteen, she was sunbathing on the roof of the pigsty. The Thames-Clyde Express was derailed a few hundred yards away. It was Eastertime, 21st April 1952. The time was 1.23 pm. Nancy heard a scraping sound and the noise of gushing steam.

'When I sat up all I could see was steam. Then I saw a locomotive on its side and three carriages lying at strange angles.'

Nancy made for the scene of the accident. She found a carry-cot containing a baby, happily unharmed. The mother scrambled out of one of the side windows of a carriage and was happily reunited with her child.

'People started coming out of the coaches. No one seemed to be badly hurt, though there were injuries caused by flying glass.'

She then found a boy who had been thrown through a window; his legs were lacerated below the knees. Other people were sitting around.

The train had almost 200 passengers. Injuries in the main were light, though seventeen passengers needed hospital treatment. The first reaction of Nancy's mum had been to 'put the kettle on for cups of tea'. She then tore sheets and pillowcases into strips to bandage up those who were bleeding.

Such was the situation of the crashed train it was some time before a rescue party arrived. The ambulance men had a shock on reaching the scene, for – as noted – it was a hot day at Easter. Passengers who were not injured were lying flat, sunbathing, their inert forms giving an impression that they were dead. Nancy received a letter of congratulations from the Girl Guides' Association and a watch from the railway authority.

Incidentally, three cranes were at the site by 5.30pm, single-line working was introduced the next day, and by 4.40pm normal service was resumed on the Settle-Carlisle line.

Station Trouble

Holiday visitor to Dent village: 'Why was Dent Station built so far from the village?'

Old man: "Appen they wanted it near t'railway.'

Dalesfolk I remember: Harry Secombe

Harry, a Welsh comedian and singer, was a dalesman for part of the day when I had the pleasure of chatting with him. We met on the 'up' platform at Settle Station. He was under the eyes of a television crew who were working on a film in the ITV series Highway. It combined interviews with local folk and some joyful hymns from Harry. He had an astonishingly loud, clear and melodic voice.

Part of the day would be spent clattering and chattering on a steam-hauled passenger train heading over embankments and viaducts in North Ribblesdale and the Eden Valley. Most of the shots of the train were from the air. It temporarily vanished, leaving a cloud of smoke, as it ran into Blea Moor Tunnel. It roused dale-country echoes with its haunting steam whistle.

Harry was a joyful man who asked a range of questions. I had recorded, and occasionally played, his visit to my favourite island, Lindisfarne, off the Northumbrian coast. Now I was going to be able to see the streamlined locomotive and its carriages from on high.

Our conversation took place twixt Settle and Appleby. He was keen to know about Ribblehead Viaduct. I mentioned that when the line became operative the Midland company permitted a harmonium to be played in the Ribblehead waiting room, where services might be held. Interludes were cut into the film of the train to permit musical items to be included. Harry's songs must have roused the echoes in the dale country. His voice lives on in the DVD that is a vivid record of the day he caught the spirit of the celebrated railway line, through chats and songs.

Return Ticket

Old John, hurrying towards the railway station, was overtaken by a younger neighbour.

'Hey Fred,' he called, 'will ta book me a return ticket?'

'Wheer to?' asked Fred.

'Back 'ere, yer fooil.'

Sir Harry Secombe

Climb Every Mountain

Coast to Coast

The walk was completed in two halves due to Dad having triple bypass surgery in the middle! This extract, written by Dad, describes the closing stages.

12th May 1995: Blakey to Grosmont

Overnight snow gives a light covering by dawn. At 6:10 a ring ouzel, the white-bibbed 'mountain blackbird', lands on a table outside the hotel and soon a skylark is heard singing. We then hear the melancholic twin-notes of a golden plover from the moor. A bumble bee flies past the window so yesterday's cold snap has not killed them all.

Colin and I find the visits of the ouzels of abiding interest. This species is usually reported from above the 1,000-feet contour. The ouzels operate a shuttle-system with worms, presumably feeding young in a nest on the nearby moor. The characteristics when food-hunting are those of the blackbird – head to one side as bird listens, jabbing the ground where the worm is to be found, then the use of claws into the ground to give stability as it pulls a worm clear. One worm appears to stretch for six inches before it is clear.

Bob and Stan were so cramped in their room they wanted us to believe that each got a leg in the same pyjama trousers and that, although the bags could be moved into the room, there was no space to open them.

The young woman who served breakfast commutes to the Lion from Easington. Her wedding took place in the dining room, with the local vicar officiating. She intended shortly to ride a horse along the Coast to Coast, raising money for charity. A most unusual lass.

We walk along the moorland road to where the skyline is dominated by Ralph Cross [the most famous of the ancient stone crosses and boundary markers on the North York Moors]. From here we glimpse the sea, about Whitby. Birds seen include ring ouzel, snipe, golden plover and red grouse. A second moorland marker, known as Fat Betty, has been given a coat of white paint.

We are all surprised and delighted by the beauty of Great Fryup Dale and Glaisdale, both extending on the southern side of Eskdale. Moorland tracks were used for the ponies transporting coal from the shafts which are widespread. We follow a ridge path with moorland on either side. The sky, with its multi-layer cumulus, extends over vast distances.

Bill shows much interest in a roadside marker with the inscription 'Whitby Road'. For this is a stone in its original socket. So great has been the erosion over the centuries that the headpiece is now chocked to prevent it moving unduly in its stone basin. Bill finds a new penny on top and adds another, then two more from passing visitors and eventually three more from the lads. A new North Yorkshire custom has been born!

We call at Glaisdale Station for tea and toasted teacake. Stan, ever alert to the presence of fine old clocks, asks the proprietor what is wrong with the one that has a prominent place in the café. The owner replies, 'It's like all the bloody clocks in this house – it wants winding up!'

We cross Beggar's Bridge and watch Colin do a walking-on-the-water act at the nearby ford. We tour yet another floriferous wood and examine some floriferous grass road verges. One notable plant was an early purple orchis. At Egton Bridge, we cross two lots of stepping stones, notice a Wellingtonia, remark on the likeness of a dog at the 'big hoose' to Mrs Pomphrey's in the James Herriot stories and then pat a goat before following a former toll road through to Grosmont.

We are in time to watch the departure of the last train, hauled by REPTON, and the return of the last train from Pickering (ERIC TREACY). Bill arranges with the Fat Controller that he will not slyly video him if he will make a personalised announcement mentioning Bob Swallow. He does. Bob looks suitably amused.

13th May: Grosmont to Robin Hood's Bay

Sunshine. Dawn chorus is a solo, from a duck. We follow Bob to the station and photograph trains. Thence up a 1-in-3 bank, on the last lap to Robin Hood's Bay. The moors are littered with stones. Also the odd tumulus. Lots of grouse are seen. We cross the Whitby road at the head of Blue Bank and examine a line of stones which is not from the 'remote mists of antiquity', being what remains of a sheepfold. We trudge down to the erstwhile quiet hamlet of Littlebeck. There is much noise, ranging from duckly quacking to a three-decibel squeal from a specialist vehicle associated with some improvement work at the old home of Thomas Whitaker. We heard that Whitaker, the wood carver, had died three years ago. An invasion of Scouts and schoolchildren adds to the confusion. We do have a butty and are amazed at the friendliness/cheek of the ducks. When all has been eaten, they begin to worry banana skins.

To the woods! We see the Hermitage [dating from as far back as the eighteenth century, it was once the secluded home of a hermit], cut out of living rock and full of excited schoolchildren, before pressing on to Falling Foss. When eventually we break out of tree cover at a car park, we are entertained by bold chaffinches and a timid robin. Both are duly 'caught' on video film. Over Greystone Hills. A quick half-pint at Hawsker and a quick walk through a caravan site and we are at the sea-cliffs.

At Robin Hood's Bay we descend the hill to the landing and allow a lively tide to partly fill our boots. Here, too, the pebbles collected on the St Bees beach a year before are ritualistically chucked into the sea. That evening, at the Victoria Hotel, the celebratory dinner took place by candlelight and eventually moonlight. We sipped mushroom soup, had glasses of wine and champed our way through the main course – Devon sole (Bob), haddock (Colin), each fish crisply golden in batter and looking a yard long. Bill had his sirloin steak well done. Stan asked for his steak to be 'cooked till it's black and the chef threatens to leave'.

Epilogue:
We awake to the clarion call of roof-nesting herring gulls, tour the old town and have a light lunch before departing for home. As Bill wrote in innumerable visitors' books: 'It's bin 'aw reet.'

Coast to Coast – View from Wainstones

Cleveland Way

The Geriatric Blunderers navigate the Cleveland Way. Dad recorded the journey and this extract describes progress on the first day, Friday 12th May 2000.

A high-speed crossing of Yorkshire, via Bedale and Thirsk, sees Bob overtaking owt that's going, including a bus on the steep part of Sutton Bank. Bill's car is left near the information centre. Bob's car is driven to the actual start at Helmsley. The pay-machine has advanced technology – far too advanced for the average motorist who waits until a whizz-kid turns up to say it's simple. We actually have the classic two-car job, dividing the walk into segments and leaving one car at each day's destination. Only Bob seems to know how the system works. Stan has been continually bemused by it. Bill, as usual, switches his mind into neutral and leaves it to the others.

The walking part of the day begins at 11:30. We follow a gently ascending track from Helmsley with Colin saying, at five-minute intervals, 'there's a good view of the castle'. He must be a shareholder in Kodak. We have a wooded gorge on our left. The song of the chiffchaff is heard. A millipede on the path is overtaken because it has a poor sense of direction and is going in the wrong direction for our next venue, Rievaulx.

Bill (left) and the Geriatric Blunderers

Colin points out Griff Lodge, Bob observes at 12:15 that we have not stopped for a drink. He stops to photograph a bluebell, one of ten million in a local wood. We walk through a pinewood. The trees are well-spaced, the ground completely carpeted by wood sorrel, the air shivering to the song of the willow warbler. Bob intones the name of local plants: primrose, garlic, herb robert, bugle, stichwort, speedwell, pink campion, crossword and tufted vetch.

We stroll beside the River Rye to Rievaulx Abbey, once a place of quaintness and reflection and now an English Heritage honeypot. A posh young lady with clapboard and notes passes us by. People are going through the entrance, to be charged, persuaded to buy books and generally harassed. We all remember when one might clamber about the ruins.

We have a butty stop by the river, the banks of which are white with garlic. Bob, who by this time has a stomach that is ringing up his brain to inquire if his throat has been cut, drinks and eats himself into a jolly mood. We stop to admire a cottage by the bridge. It has a garden of the chocolate box type. The view is fringed by white and pink blossoms from roadside trees. We stroll through Nettledale (a message on a gate reads: Private Road. Adders on Bank Sides) and Flassendale

(pheasants in profusion). Colin: 'I feel a snooze coming on.'

We see a riverbank patched with the gold of marsh marigold. In the old woodland are tracts of anemones. Primroses grow profusely on earthen banks. Dog violet is common. Wild strawberry is in flower.

We have a stiffish climb to where the land plateaus (Colin's expression) and skylarks are singing over miles of arable crops – all of the same tedious shade of green. Gobbling turkeys, all white, are passing the time until gobbling will relate not to the sound they make but Christmas feasting. A pair of lapwings is seen. Swifts skate about the sunlit sky.

At Cold Kirby, which is almost literally two rows of pantile-roofed cottages looking at each other over several hundred yards of ground and with a church at one end, we ate our butties sitting on a wall, watching the local sparrows have dust baths. We are on the 1000 foot contour, says Colin. Bill reports the passage of a small tortoiseshell butterfly.

There is now evidence of the Yorkshire Gliding Club's activities at Sutton Bank. A light aircraft is towing a glider to a height where it might loiter on the upthrust of air from the escarpment (or summat). As we approach the car park at the end of the day's walking. Bill films an adder. It is young, bears the dark zig-zag of its kind and has just eaten judging by the mid-length swelling which is about mouse-size.

We drive back to Helmsley for Bob's car, then take both cars to our lodging for the next five nights – namely 4 Manor Grove, Great Broughton (pronounced Browton by the locals). We stayed here for a night on the Coast to Coast Walk. We had a happy reunion with Ron and Jean Noble. Ron lapses into local talk, mentioning Chop Yat (Chop Gate), Cannie Yatton (Great Ayton) and using the words 'yep', 'aye' and 'well' as verbal fill-ups, which is the Dales way of keeping a conversation going.

17th May: The views of the coast are far-ranging and fascinating. Container ships are waiting for the right stage of the tide before entering the Tyne. We are overtaken by a lady rambler with tinted hair and a straight neck. She does not pause for an instant, intent on reaching her destination. We reach the summit of the cliff near Boulby which is the highest point on the English coast. At Staithes we venture on to Cowbar Nab, following a path between ranks of gorse and cow parsley to the rim of the cliff where herring gulls are shouting at each other – and maybe also at us. Bill chats with a man wearing red throughout from bobble-cap to breeks. He points out

where his son is working on a boat, using the name Baldy – 'but don't use that name to his face!'

We crossed to Runswick Bay, having wide views of the sea, which has never impressed Stan. He says it is so flat! At the Bay, we marvel at the changes wrought by a £3m scheme that has turned a sloping car park into a level one, has reinforced the coastline with large, alien boulders and created a new café, which we patronised, while retaining the little thatched cottage by the sea.

Our route lay across the sands (dwindling with the flow tide). Through a gorge and up several flights of steps leading to the clifftop. The steps changed in character, from some with beaten earth to others that were green from an invasion of grass. At each stage we could look across the bay at Runswick, a huddle of red-roofed buildings perched on sloping ground above the sea.

And of course, there was the prospect of being near the railway. Bob, with confident expectation, almost took root while waiting for a train to arrive. There was no train as such, just a big diesel locomotive using a historic sea-edge track which at one time included a mile long tunnel driven through rock. Bob came into his own as raconteur when Kettleness station was reached. We had just seen

Kettleness Rock, mainly naked rock, jutting far into the North Sea.

So we came to Sandsend. We collected Bob's car then went for Bill's at Skinningrove. The bonnets of the cars were now turned towards Robin Hood's Bay where we would spend our last two nights. We used 'digs' we had visited during the Coast to Coast Walk and also dined at the Victoria Hotel, at that time using a dining room that looked out over the bay where we had seen the sun rise. After our evening meal, we went outside to see the sun riding high over the bay which was delineated by a silver sheen. Luvly!

18th May: To Ravenscar with Bob's car. As we drew to a halt quite early in the day we saw two roe deer cavorting on a grassy area. They slipped over the edge of the cliff, descending to the vast undercliff, where there is both cover and good browsing for deer.

We walked from the car park at Sandsend, passing Whitby golf course, where the play was rather less than moderate in quality and Bob was shaken to find the remnant of the railway embankment being used for teeing off. Signs warned us of truant golf balls. On the West Cliff at Whitby we saw the Arnold Palmer putting course. So much for commercialisation.

Whitby was not as Bill remembered it – bright, red-roofed with a sparkle on the harbour but lacking the row of keel boats that once gave the quayside interest and colour. Also, the modern obsession with *Dracula* because the novelist chose to set the early part in Whitby, which has for long until recently been a God-fearing place. Seeing the parish church on the cliff-top, Bill was reminded of an old-time notice: No Camping in the Churchyard.

As we strode from Whitby towards Ravenscar, with a view from the cliff of Saltwick Nab, the heavens opened and we eventually scuttered for a shelter at a caravan park. We plodded on, getting wet, and when a dry spell came we stopped for a butty and hung our wet anoraks on the 'finger' of a direction post, hoping they would drip-dry.

The cliff edge path led us t'Hawsker bull, a fog horn near a lighthouse. The cliff was colonised by noisy kittiwakes and silent fulmars. We selected the old trail track in preference to the now slippery clay path near the sea. Beyond Robin Hood's Bay, the track petered out and notices directed us along a detour which proved difficult to understand and potentially hazardous. In due course, we were back on track and completed the journey to Ravenscar with stiffening legs and in relatively dry conditions.

My Yorkshire…WR MITCHELL
Interview from the *Yorkshire Post*

What's your first memory of being outdoors?

A moorland walk, Skipton to the village of Bradley, with my father. He had a habit of sipping chilled water from the spring he had dreamed about while hospitalised with a fever in Malta during the First World War when he served with the Royal Navy.

What's your favourite part of the county and why?

Upper Wharfedale, varied and romantic.

Do you have a favourite view?

The precipitous north-face of Ingleborough, 'big blue hill', framed by the lych gate at Chapel-le-Dale churchyard. Ruskin marvelled that Ingleborough, beset by a strong wind, managed to stand without rocking.

Which Yorkshire sportsman/ sportswomen (past or present) would you like to take for lunch?

My old friend, John Rawnsley, of Three Peaks cyclo-cross fame, who has often completed the 25-mile circuit, sometimes riding, sometimes running with the bike over his shoulder.

Which Yorkshire stage or screen star (past or present) would you like to take for lunch?

Richard Whiteley. We swapped stories. He told me of addressing a vast crowd in Bradford. He shouted at them: 'Can you all hear me?' A man sitting half way down the hall shouted back: 'I can but I don't mind changing places with someone who can't.'

If you had to name your Yorkshire hidden gem, what would it be?

Cotter Force, reached by a short cul-de-sac footpath signposted at the side of the main road where it straightens out after crossing the bridge beyond Appersett in Wensleydale. The Cotter pours over a broad lip of limestone, in summer under a proscenium arch of greenery.

What do you think gives Yorkshire its unique identity?

Scenic variety. The Plain of York is like the palm of a hand, from which finger-like dales extend westwards. In contrast is the crescent of chalk, forming the Wolds, which has its seaward termination in the dazzling white cliffs of Flamborough and Bempton.

What about Yorkshire's cultural life?

Rich and varied, especially in music, from brass bands to massed voices. My favourite Yorkshire composer is Arthur Wood, born in Heckmondwike. He played a flute for chapel concerts and composed the Maypole dance, Barwick Green in My Native Heath. For years it has provided a popular radio series, The Archers, with a lively musical introduction.

Do you have a favourite restaurant or pub?

Since Freda, my wife of 55 years, died last July, I vary microwaved food and cheese on toast with a visit to Settle Down in town – local food, freshly cooked, plus an update, through chats with friends, on local gossip. For novelty value, I patronise the café at Hellifield Railway Station, an island station, the platforms of which are approached by subway. In the café you might simultaneously sip tea and watch trains, which pass on either side of what was formerly the restaurant room. Bliss.

How do you think Yorkshire has changed in the time you've known it?

The traditional life has been diluted and given a thick crust of bureaucracy. Newcomers have contributed a lot but have much more to learn; they'd look askance if you talked about being 'as dry as a lime-burner's clog' or 'as handy as t'dish clout'.

Are these changes for the better?

Social life is much more varied than it was. And more entertaining. Who'd have thought, years ago, when devout folk used to cover up the bare legs of the table on a Sunday, that members of a dale-country Women's Institute would strip for a calendar photograph?

Who is the Yorkshire man or woman you most admire?

Bob Swallow, a walking companion in Yorkshire and Lakeland for well over thirty years. We are disciples of Wainwright, members of a quartet known as The Geriatric Blunderers (president: Betty Wainwright; motto: 'you name it, we've been lost on it'). Bob has some funny expressions. If a bad day improves weatherwise, it's getting less worse!

How has Yorkshire influenced your work?

Yorkshire is my work. I enjoy writing about it and its people. I like to keep busy. As they say in Yorkshire: 'T'hardest wark is doin' nowt'.

Name your favourite Yorkshire book.

The Yorkshire Dales, Marie Hartley and Joan Ingilby. Factual, readable and with that rare and delicate element we used to know as charm.

Acknowledgements

Sincere thanks to the following:
The *Craven Herald* for permission to use extracts from Bill's regular
articles for the newspaper's history pages
Yorkshire Post for permission to use articles and feature a 'My Yorkshire'
interview, with questions by Mick Hickling, from May 2008
Sita Brand, Settle Stories, for use of photographs and permission to
feature extracts from the WR Mitchell Archive
Settle and District Community News
Great Northern Books
Additional pictures: Adrian Braddy, Richard Littlewood,
freeimageslive.co.uk, photoeverywhere, Welcome to Yorkshire

Page References

Foreword: My Yorkshire, *Dalesman* 1993

FAMILY AND ROOTS: p12 Life in't back street, Indepenpress 2013;
p14 A Yorkshire courtship, Indepenpress, 2011; p16 From the Yorkshire
Dales to Salt Lake City, Indepenpress 2012; p18 Looking for Grandad,
2008

HERALDING A CAREER FOR THE DALESMAN: p19 Ink on my
fingers, from *Settle & District Community News* June 2008; p22 A Dales
Editor, *Dalesman* April 1993; p24 Tales of a dryland sailor, date unknown;
p26 Homely beginnings with the great Scotts, *Dalesman* May 1998

PEOPLE BEFORE THINGS: p29 Old Mick the bull walloper, *Dalesman*
October 1949; p32 Annie Mason, interview 1988 – from the WR
Mitchell Archive; p34 Dalesfolk I remember: Bill Alderson, *Dalesman*
December 2014; p36 Kit Calvert, from *How they Lived In The Yorkshire
Dales*, Castleberg 2001; p41 Hannah's Christmas, *Dalesman* December

1979; p43 Life and times of Tot Lord, *Dalesman* May 1986; p45 Tot Tommy, *Dalesman* September 1981; p46 Tommy Moore: the complete dalesman, *Dalesman* February 1999; p48 Sally's parrot, *Settle Community News* February 2010

FAR FROM THE MADDING CROWD: p49 Sad day as bus company completes its final journey, *Craven Herald* May 2014; p52 A postman's life, from *Nobbut Middlin'*, Castleberg 2000; p55 A taste of some old-fashioned medicine, *Yorkshire Post* March 2008; p56 A Dales tailor, *Dalesman* April 1998; p58 Broadcasting in the Broad Acres, *Craven Herald* September 2014; p60 Tales about babyhood, *Settle and District Community News* June 2011

TRADITIONS: p61 Showtime at Muker, *Dalesman* January 1987; p64 Dancing in the Dales, *Dalesman* May 1982 & from *Letters from the Dales*, Castleberg 1994; p66 Last of the 'terrible' knitters, from *Letters from the Dales*, Castleberg 1994 & *Music of the Yorkshire Dales*, Castleberg 1997; p68 Dales tales of a Christmas past, *Dalesman* December 1998; p71 First footing at White Scar, *Dalesman* January 1989 & from *Summat and Nowt* Castleberg 2000; p72 Lecturer's magic lantern effect that brought nature to life, *Craven Herald* May 2010;

YORKSHIRE'S SCENIC VARIETY: p73 White walls of Yorkshire, *Dalesman* November 1977 & 'My Yorkshire', *Dalesman* 1993; p77 Nineteen forty-seven, *Dalesman* 2007; p79 Tour brings thoughts of the past, *Craven Herald* August 2014; p81 Shuttle service to the underworld, *Dalesman* February 1994; p83 Drystone walls add to Dales landscape, *Craven Herald* February 2015; p86 A corner of Yorkshire: Goathland, *Yorkshire Post* June 2008; p87 Ilkley Moor Baht 'at, 'My Yorkshire', *Dalesman* 1993; p89 A corner of Yorkshire: Janet's Foss, *Yorkshire Post* May 2008

HISTORY: p90 Looking for Lady Anne, *Dalesman* December 1990; p94 The Romantics and the Dales, *Craven Herald* October 2015

ARTS: p95 JB in the Dales, *Dalesman* September 2014; p97 Great-great Grandad knew the Brontës, *Craven Herald*, December 2009; p99 Young Mr Herriot, *Dalesman*, February 1990; p103 Christopher Timothy on location, *Dalesman* May 2014; p105 Cutcliffe Hyne: a huge man, mentally and physically, *Dalesman*, Volume 17 1955; p107 Chapters in a Dales life, from *Letters from the Dales*, Castleberg 1994; p111 Elgar's friendship with a Yorkshire doctor, *Dalesman* December 1978; p112 The clouds are mucky: Ashley Jackson, *Dalesman* July 1993; p116 Fred Lawson, from *How they Lived in the Yorkshire Dales* Castleberg 2001 & *Summat and Nowt*, Castleberg 1998; p117 At home with Thelma Barlow, *Dalesman* February 1987

WILDLIFE/NATURE: p118 Richard Kearton, *Dalesman*, April/May 1977; p120 Legacy of Yorkshire's natural history boys, *Yorkshire Post*, January 2008; p123 Evenings with barn owls, from *Letters from the Dales*, Castleberg 1994; p125 The farming family who built up a stock of deer, *Craven Herald* October 2013; p127 Gardening's own rock legend, *Yorkshire Post* May 2007

THERE'S METHODISM IN MY MADNESS: p129 Pulpit tales of the Yorkshire Dales, Indepenpress 2013; p130 Old-style Methodism, from *Letters from the Dales*, Castleberg 1994, 'Chapel Tales' in *Settle Community News* June 2009 & *Nobbut Middlin'*, Castleberg 2000; p132 Mr Parker's favourite hymn, *Dalesman* December 1991

SUFFERING FROM SETTLE-CARLITIS: p134 The railway in the clouds, from *Letters from the Dales*, Castleberg 1994; p135 The runaway, from *One Hundred Tales of the Settle-Carlisle Railway*; p138 A quest for the shanties, *Dalesman* February 1978; p143 When the Scots Express left the rails, from *Thunder in the Mountains*, Great Northern Books 2009; p144 Dalesfolk I remember: Harry Secombe, *Dalesman* November 2014

CLIMB EVERY MOUNTAIN...: p146 Coast to Coast, May 1995; p149 Cleveland Way, May 2000

MY YORKSHIRE: WR MITCHELL p155 Interview with Mick Hickling, *Yorkshire Post* May 2008